Human Resource Management

To M-J

TONY SADLER

Human Resource Management

Developing a STRATEGIC

———————— APPROACH

**KOGAN
PAGE**

YOURS TO HAVE AND TO HOLD
BUT NOT TO COPY

First published in 1995

Kogan Page Limited
120 Pentonville Road
London N1 9JN

© Tony Sadler, 1995

British Library Cataloguing in Publication Data

A CIP record for this book is available from the British Library.

ISBN 0 7494 1509 6

Typeset by DP Photosetting, Aylesbury, Bucks
Printed in England by Clays Ltd, St Ives plc

Contents

Acknowledgements

This is essentially a practical book, and I have drawn from my experience of the art and science of personnel management over some 30 years. I have learned something of what I know from books and articles, and much from actually doing the work day by day. But I have also benefited enormously from the help, guidance and wisdom of many colleagues and friends – some of them my bosses over the years and some of them members of my team or peers – and if there is anything of value in this book I owe it mostly to them. I thank them all.

Some I would particularly like to acknowledge. The first company I joined as a raw graduate was then known as the De Havilland Aircraft Company – a name to conjure with for those whose memories go back that far. This was one of those exemplary companies which provided a wonderful training ground for personnel managers. I am greatly indebted to my bosses and mentors in those days, especially to the, to my callow youth, fairly fearsome Bob Cooper, to John Maynard, who taught me a lot as well as protecting me somewhat from Bob, and to Ray Lupini, who first persuaded me to join him in personnel.

Later, I was offered a job in the Rank Organisation by another graduate of the De Havilland school, Derek Walker. Derek proved to be another wonderful mentor and friend, and gave me the opportunity to become involved in the international scene.

These were the action players. I am also grateful to some of the thinkers in our profession, and in particular to Edwin Singer, who knows almost everything there is to know about coaching, and taught me some of it, and to Ian Hinton, who has been a superb mentor to me in the Coverdale traditions of management training and development. Ian is also famous for his recipe for rum punch!

Personnel is about the importance of people in organisations and I have learned much about the full dimensions of humanity from my old friend, Owen Swann. From him, I have understood something of the interplay between the sacred and the secular.

When contemplating the possibility of writing this book, I was introduced to Pauline Goodwin of Kogan Page, and am grateful to her for her encouragement. Once the book was written, I was delighted that Chris Stephens took on the task of reading it and commenting on it from the point of view of the experienced professional.

Finally, I am indebted to all those companies and other organisations whose policies and practice are cited in the book. Personnel management is to some degree under attack, but there are many personnel professionals involved in first class pioneering work. I would not wish to single out any companies in particular, but all the names are included in the index.

Tony Sadler

Introduction
The Opportunity and the Challenge

This book is driven by the conviction that the personnel function could, and should, be making a bigger contribution to business than is currently the case. When asked where they would like to be in two years' time compared to today, many personnel professionals will respond with words such as 'well, I would like to be more clearly a part of the management team' or, in the same vein, 'more involved in management decisions'. The purpose of this book is to help them to be just that.

Of course there are exceptions, cases where the function is making a first rate contribution to the organisation and its investment in the human resource. Many instances are included in the book by way of illustration. Yet it is usually just those excellent exemplars who are the first to recognise that we all still have much to learn in the art and science of managing people well. Continuous improvement is clearly one of the hallmarks of world class companies and individuals. In this spirit of sharing experience and best practice there will hopefully be worthwhile things in the book even for those who would regard themselves as 'state of the art' practitioners.

One of the themes of the book is change. The way organisations work, indeed their very purpose, is evolving with astonishing rapidity. This is creating a big challenge for personnel management; in fact, its very existence as a viable function is threatened. Yet at the same time these changes present us with a new opportunity to make a really substantial impact.

So the book is by way of an exploration – how can we as personnel professionals move beyond the administrative and reactive environment which so often binds us, to seize the strategic opportunities so nearly within our grasp? There are no easy answers, and some clear thinking and not a little determination are required. What we do know is that if we do not make a start we will be no further forward in two years' time than we are now – and may well have gone backwards. Conversely, if we start down the road, we may surprise ourselves – the reward will be considerable not only to our organisations, but also in terms of our own satisfaction and development.

Our exploration needs to be in some sort of context. So, Chapter 1 provides by way of background and introduction a brief overview of current thinking about business strategy in general. Chapters 2 and 3 review the main people issues in contemporary organisations, and discuss how the distinct roles of line management and the personnel specialist work together to tackle these issues.

Like all aspects of business, the personnel function needs to relate decisively to customers. Chapter 4 focuses on our customers, and suggests a new alliance between personnel and marketing. Customer service is an essential value in most organisations, but what are the other values that drive policy, practice and behaviour? Chapter 5 explores the concept that strategy is 'values driven' – what is, or should be, the contribution of personnel in this area?

All this is vital ground for any personnel practitioner seeking to get to grips with his or her strategic role. The second half of the book offers a series of models and ideas designed to lead to action. Chapter 6 builds up a practical model for developing a human resources (HR) strategy and the following chapter relates this to some specific functional areas, such as employee relations, compensation and benefits, and training and development.

Chapter 8 offers some thinking about the role of the HR director, and about what training and development is required to prepare for such a role. What are the important competences? What makes for success in the role?

Finally, by definition the strategic approach involves looking ahead to take account of likely future developments. We must guard against being inward looking and short term. Even as we catch up with what the world demands of us today, new issues of fundamental importance are just around the corner. Chapter 9 looks at some future perspectives, which point to the shape of things to come.

I wish to tackle head on the issue of personnel versus HR. In some circles this has been the subject of heated debate. Human resource management (HRM) has been seen as an attempt by management, perhaps more specifically in the US, to circumvent union recognition by the use of so-called HR techniques. On the other hand, in an article based on the HRRC Report for 1994,[1] Professor Shaun Tyson refers to practices applying to the employment relationship. He comments 'whether this is called "human resource management" or "personnel management" is a debate which has largely occupied academics, but which seems increasingly irrelevant to practitioners.'

Irrelevant or not, in a book such as this, we need to be clear on the definitions to be used. And in fact I would like to enter the lists on the matter. I would suggest that there is a useful differentiation to be made between the two terms, but not along the lines of HRM versus IR. Rather, human resource management should be seen as that part of overall managerial responsibilities dealing with the people dimension. Personnel on the other hand is the title to be given to the specific professional function which makes a distinctive contribution to management in this field. This approach has the advantage of recognising the fact that all managers have people responsibilities, while not confusing this with the role of personnel. It also enables us to draw a distinction between the personnel manager, responsible for managing the personnel department, and the individual board member with a responsibility for human resource management in its widest sense, who will properly have the title of HR director.

There is a reasonable analogy here with finance and accountancy. All managers have some responsibility for finance, and the board member with that particular portfolio is usually called finance director. On the hand, the professionals and the professional institute use the term accountancy.

Whether such a distinction will commend itself to readers in any general way remains to be seen, but in any event this is the way the terms will be deployed here.

I try in this book to maintain a balance between the thinking which needs to underpin what we do, and the action which alone gives real results at the end of the day. To help you to do the same, each chapter concludes with a summary and *some key questions*. The questions for this Introduction are in the box below.

> **Key questions**
>
> - What do you hope to get out of this book?
> - Where do you hope to be in two years' time?
> - Have you a clear and realistic plan to get there?

Notes

1. Tyson, Shaun and Witcher, Michael (1994) 'Getting in Gear; Post-Recession HR Management,' *Personnel Management*, August, pp 20–3.

Part One

Personnel and the Meaning of Strategy

Many organisations, and individuals, are currently so caught up in immediate issues that talk about strategy seems unrealistic. One hears comments such as 'Yes, we have a strategy – to survive to the end of next week!'

In fact, strategy *is* about survival because a business that merely concerns itself with today will not last long. And so it is with individuals within the business. We all need to equip ourselves for what lies ahead – adopt in fact a strategy of lifelong learning.

Any personnel practitioner who is serious about adopting a strategic approach needs to have a grasp of what strategic thinking is. How do business leaders and thinkers see strategy in the contemporary scene? How has this evolved? Where do we go from here?

The ambition of many of us has been to work in an organisation where there is a real commitment to the fundamental importance of people. This has often appeared to be a pipe dream: when the chips are down, other things come first. Is this still the case or is there a real sea change on the horizon?

If there is a better understanding that people make the difference, what are the implications for personnel? What is the nature of such a challenge and are we ready and able to respond?

1
Strategy – What Is It?

"If you don't know where you're goin', you'll end up someplace else!"
Casey Stengel, American baseball star

A STARTING POINT

'Strategy' is one of those words that is bandied about on management courses, with sometimes not too much care as to definition. It derives from the military sphere and this is clear from dictionary definitions. *The Chambers 20th Century Dictionary* describes it as 'generalship, or the art of conducting a campaign', while *The Oxford English Dictionary* is equally direct – 'The art of a Commander in Chief'. This tells us two things: strategy is certainly about leadership, and is more concerned with the broad direction of affairs than detailed implementation. In thinking about battles to come, Wellington is reported to have spoken admiringly of French troops: 'they have besides a new system of strategy which has out-manoeuvred and overwhelmed all the armies of Europe'. However good your troops and your tactical movements, effective strategy is essential to success in the military sphere.

Yet how applicable is this to business affairs? Some decades ago, long term planning was a vogue phrase, and corporations set up substantial departments devoted to this activity. These have long since been abandoned, together with their plans, many of which simply gathered dust within corporate head office. The pendulum of opinion has swung to the other extreme in some quarters, where we are told that 'We don't know what is going to happen next week, let alone in five years' time!' This is not a particularly attractive option, implying as it does that business is entirely at the mercy of external economic and other forces. It means that all we can do is react and hope for the best, an approach that is at the opposite extreme to any kind of strategic thinking. That much quoted manual on business strategy, Lewis Carroll's *Alice's Adventures in Wonderland* has something to say on the subject:

Alice: 'Would you tell me, please, which way I ought to go from here?'
Cheshire Cat: 'That depends a good deal on where you want to get to.'
Alice: 'I don't much care where . . .'
Cheshire Cat: 'Then it doesn't matter which way you go'.

THE RATIONALIST SCHOOL

It is instructive to look briefly at the way management thinking has developed over the last 30 years. Strategy has been one of the main areas of interest to both academics and consultants since the 1960s, an early example being Peter Drucker's famous question, 'what business are you in?' The development of an effective strategy was seen not only as of key importance to business success, but also as a way of establishing management control, particularly in the vast corporations which were being created. If management was a science, it should surely be possible to identify underlying laws and principles, and bring mathematical and other tools of logic to bear. This kind of thinking led to the creation of what has been called the 'rationalist school'.

Because it was assumed that strategy had to stem essentially from a rational and planned base, corporate planning and budgetary control departments seemed to provide the obvious starting point. However, it became apparent that much of this kind of work was somehow apart from the realities of everyday business, and the great reports emanating from these departments lacked credibility.

Such corporate planning was not enough because it did not respond to change. So a new approach evolved, based on analysing all the factors making up the environment in which the business was operating, to determine strategy in the light of that analysis and then to plan implementation.

During the '70s and '80s, much work was done to produce models to facilitate this rational process. Some of this work emanated from the major consulting groups, such as the Boston Consulting Group, with its symbols of stars and dogs and cash cows. Other influential work was promulgated by individuals, such as Porter with his concept of 'the value chain', and Peters and Waterman, who conceived the implementation of strategy as a balance between 'breaking old habits', 'stability', and 'entrepreneurship'.

Another important attempt to bring a systematic and logical approach to bear on the development and implementation of strategy was made by Kepner and Tregoe. Indeed, their best known book has the title *The Rational Manager*. They see strategy in terms of an organisation's basic purpose, and as 'the framework which guides those choices that determine its nature and direction'. They make a clear distinction between strategy and long-range planning and the difference is highly instructive. Long-range planning suggests a five-year forecast related to the present day. But in his study with John Zimmerman, Benjamin Trego[1] asks how this will work without a structured framework for looking ahead five years. Without such a framework, managers have no option but to fall back on extrapolations from the current year's data. What then happens is that this year's projections are firmly fixed as a budget, while the following years are modified in line with results.

Rational strategy, on the other hand, offers a more dynamic framework. For example, a key concept within the Kepner–Tregoe approach is the 'identification, management and resolution of . . . Critical Issues'.

NEW THINKING

All this work aimed to bring rationality and logical process to bear on the task of devising and implementing strategy. The more recent work of Henry Mintzberg, an academic from McGill University, in a sense takes this process further, but also points to a less formal and even opportunistic approach.[2] For a start, he recognises that we tend to use the word strategy in different ways, suggesting a more diverse definition of the word. He proposes that we look at five definitions, and their interrelationships, and chooses words beginning with the same letter – plan, ploy, pattern, position, and perspective. So, in many situations, 'strategy is a plan – some sort of consciously intended course of action . . .' Used in the sense of ploy, strategy is a manoeuvre to outwit an opponent. The notion of 'pattern' applies where we find 'consistency in behaviour'. This leads us to ask whether the pattern arises because of a predetermined plan. Mintzberg decides that in practice this is not necessarily the case, and he distinguishes between 'deliberate' strategies and 'emergent' ones.

His concept of strategy as 'position' links directly with a further definition in *Chambers* – 'strategic position – a position that gives its holder a decisive advantage'.

Finally, Mintzberg uses the word 'perspective'. This looks inside an organisation, at, as it were, its personality. Here, what is important about strategy is that people in the organisation share the same perspective. The writer discusses 'how intentions become shared, and how action comes to be exercised on a collective yet consistent basis'.

It is significant that so far it has been assumed that strategies will be established in writing, whereas it is clear that Mintzberg envisages that this will not always be the case. In fact, his research reveals some kinds of organisations where strategy lies almost exclusively in the mind of the chief executive. In such organisations, strategy tends to be 'highly intuitive and nonanalytical, often thriving on uncertainty, and oriented to the aggressive search for opportunities'. It tends to start with a broad vision of the business – strategy as perspective.

Mintzberg starts the process of drawing away from the idea that the formulation of strategy is essentially a rational and formalised procedure. Others take this even further. Among them is Professor Brian Quinn, who has coined the phrase 'logical incrementalism'.[3] For him, strategy proceeds 'flexibly and experimentally' from broad concept to particular commitment, using delay to acquire more information and thus reduce risks. It typically evolves from consensus among top management, created by interaction between internal decisions and external events. It recognises 'soft' issues, not susceptible to quantitative techniques, such as employee relationships and management style. Quinn draws attention to what he calls 'precipitating events' – events outside management's control which could precipitate 'urgent piecemeal interim decisions that inexorably shaped the company's future strategic posture'.

From his study of nine major corporations, Quinn concluded that most effective strategies of major enterprises tend to emerge from an iterative process. These allow the enterprise to learn more about what is the unknowable future. Quinn is at pains to point out that this is not merely muddling through – it is 'a conscious purposeful proactive executive practice'.

This radically different way of looking at strategy is derived in part from an appreciation of the speed of change in our contemporary world. Yet it also reflects a more profound reality. In his recent book *Managing to Make Organisations Work*, Barry Welch writes of the need to become 'new-minded'. He claims that 'radical change now has to embrace all aspects of managing, from interpersonal relationships to the nature of business strategy'. He quotes the philosopher–physicist Fritjof Capra. For Capra, we find ourselves:

... in a state of profound world-wide crisis: we can read about the various aspects of this crisis every day in the newspapers ... all of these threats are ... essentially a crisis of perception. We are trying to apply the concepts of an outdated world view – the mechanistic world view of Cartesian–Newtonian science – to a reality that can no longer be understood in these terms ... The beginnings of this change are already visible in all fields, and the shift from a mechanistic to a holistic conception of reality is likely to dominate the entire decade.

BUSINESS SUCCESS – BY LUCK OR JUDGMENT?

A similarly radical viewpoint has been expressed by John Kay, Professor of Economics at the London Business School:[4]

Intriguingly, it is modern developments in mathematics which have demonstrated what most practical businessmen long suspected. Attempts to forecast the evolution of a firm for more than a short period ahead are fundamentally useless. Two decades ago, it seemed possible to believe that technology would ultimately conquer these problems. With sufficient information and infinitely powerful computers, the uncertainties of business behaviour would gradually be resolved. We know now that this will never be true.

On the other hand, Kay is careful not to throw out the baby with the bathwater. Although he is clear that 'the evolution of a business can never be wholly predictable or controllable', he confirms that 'it is not a chance process either'. He uses three case studies, among others, to illustrate this thinking. The first is BMW, which Kay describes as 'a company with a well-executed strategy'. Yet this was not based on a master plan or single vision, and other options could have been chosen. The essential for Kay was that BMW came to recognise what he calls its 'distinctive capabilities', and to exploit them effectively.

His second example is Honda's entry into the US motorcycle market. Honda had originally intended to compete with the Americans on their own terms, selling 250cc and 350cc machines. In fact, they achieved success quite unexpectedly, when they realised there was a huge new market for their 50cc supercub. Kay concludes, 'like all successful strategies, it was based on a mixture of calculation and opportunism, of vision and experiment'.

The third example is a less happy one and concerns the efforts of Groupe Bull. It is true that the company had a strategic vision, spelled out by its Chief Executive in June 1989 – 'to become the major European supplier of global information systems'. Over the following years it fell deep into loss and was forced in 1992 to announce an alliance with the arch-enemy, IBM. For Kay, the problem was that the company lacked 'the distinctive capabilities which would enable it to realise that vision'. It epitomised what he calls 'wish-driven strategy, based on aspiration, not capability'. His conclusion is that 'effective strategy starts from what the company is distinctively good at, not from what it would like to be good at, and is adaptive and opportunistic in exploiting what is distinctive in these capabilities'.

The ill-fated Ryder plan for the recovery of the then British Leyland was another wish-driven strategy. Apart from anything else it required the injection of further huge tranches of taxpayers' money, a proposition that was politically a dead duck, even if it had made sound commercial and industrial sense. It was only when management started to take a realistic view of Rover's position in world markets, that recovery became a possibility. Since then, the company has demonstrated in a remarkable way what clear strategic thinking can achieve.

STRATEGY – A THINKING PROCESS

In considering how strategy is formulated within organisations, we cannot ignore the individual thinking processes of those making the key decisions. In an article in the *Harvard Business Review*, Arnoud de Meyer of INSEAD asks 'can management skills be taught and researched at all?'[4] One might think this is quite an important question for a business professor; in fact de Meyer goes further: 'do we to-day – after all the research – know more about good business management than we did 50 years ago?' He concludes that there is a place for teaching analytical skills, but that this is far from the whole answer.

During the '80s, work done by a research team within the Philips Group, led by Jerry Rhodes, focused on the way individuals think. This resulted in the development of the Thinking–Intentions Profile, described by Rhodes in his book *The Colours of Your Mind*. He contends that individuals have preferred ways of thinking, and gives each mode a colour code:

- *judgmental (blue)*, representing preference for judging what's right, based on logic, relevance, values, subjective interpretation, and past experience

- *descriptive (red)*, seeking what's true, based upon current existing information,details, explicit and implicit aspects of the situation
- *creative (green)*, thriving on the use of intuition and imagination to develop new ideas and vision.

Each type of thinking has two biases, hard and soft. Hard focuses on the external world of tangibles, soft on the inner world of intangibles.

On this analysis, different individuals will tend to approach strategy in very different ways, the naturally 'hard' thinkers emphasising management control, quantitative measures and technical analysis, with 'soft' on the other hand preferring flexibility, qualitative approaches and vision.

A current management 'guru', Richard Pascale, preaches that change is not enough. He claims that a transformation is needed, which requires a new mindset – a total paradigm shift, based on where the organisation is now and a preparedness to grapple with the unpredictable. Such a shift starts by identifying what paradigms reign currently in the firm and the forces that sustain them. He gives British Airways as an example, where the predominant way of seeing things was based on operational requirements, with passengers regarded as cargo to be transported. The transformation only took place when the need to change this was recognised and the customer moved to the forefront. It would appear that a substantial dose of 'green' thinking is essential if such transformations are to be achieved.

An impressive example of such corporate transformation is the TI Group. In 1984, the company, previously known as Tube Investments, was by its own admission a fairly unfocused UK collection of companies in the metal bashing business. In the '70s, it employed in excess of 60,000 people, almost exclusively in the UK, with a sales turnover of around £1.1 billion. Within ten years it had transformed itself into a highly profitable international business with sales of around £1.4 billion, employing around 24,000, of whom only a third work in the UK. The difference may be summarised in one word – strategy. From the time of his appointment in 1988, the then chief executive, Christopher Lewinton (now Sir Christopher) pursued a coherent strategy, based on a clear recognition of the company's strengths and the opportunities it could create in the international marketplace. The strategy statement reads:

> TI Group's strategy is to be an international engineering group concentrating on specialised engineering businesses, operating in selected niches on a global basis. Key businesses must be able to command positions of sustainable technological and market share leadership. They

will have a high knowledge and service content and will be able to anticipate and meet customers' needs.

Doubtless the road to its achievement was not without its ups and downs; nevertheless, management succeeded in engendering a process based on a realistic vision which moved the organisation forward in a highly effective way.

It is in effect more useful to think of strategic thinking as a continuing process, rather than the establishment of a fully fleshed-out plan for the next x years. Indeed, it could even be argued that the real importance lies in the quality of the thinking process itself rather than its specific outcomes at any one moment. Such a process will be constantly subject to revision and experiment in the light of changing circumstances, although holding fast to some core ideas as to what the particular business is all about.

STRATEGY AS IMPLEMENTATION

Many writers have debated whether you can separate strategy from its implementation. Kay gives the example of Napoleon's ill-fated Russian campaign. Was his defeat a failure of strategy or of implementation? Once strategy is seen essentially as process, the two elements become totally interwoven. This is perhaps especially the case where organisations are taking out layers of management and pushing decisions down the line. It is likely that in such organisations decisions with strategic implications are being taken at an increasingly junior level. One phrase to describe this process is 'strategy as an emerging process of action'. In the light of such developments it becomes critical that a sense of direction and of values is effectively communicated within the business, so that decisions with strategic implications are congruent with the direction of the whole.

A SUMMARY

We need at this stage to summarise where we have got to in this overview of thinking about strategy, and to relate the argument to the personnel function. A summary of the key points so far is as follows:

1.   There has been much work since the 1960s to answer the questions 'what is business strategy and how do we do it?' An early

assumption was that a rational study of the subject would produce a model based on sound principles which managers could learn to apply in an analytical way.

2.   This work produced a series of influential models, but we are now realising that this is only one side of the story.

3.   The reality is that organisations are faced with an increasingly unpredictable world. Change is not susceptible to a one-off programme that will lead to calmer times.

4.   Yet to survive and thrive, businesses cannot afford simply to be buffeted by uncontrollable forces, in the hope that luck will be on their side. Success will not happen by chance but through continuous strategic processes that will ride these choppy waters. (It has been said that the Japanese in top management see themselves as 'white water rafters'!)

5.   Some characteristics of these processes include:

   ● a recognition that short term decisions have long term consequences
   ● the processes are values driven
   ● strategic decisions have a sense of direction, related to a vision of what could be
   ● this 'what could be' has to be based on the distinctive capabilities of the firm – it is not just a 'wish list'
   ● strategic decisions have implications for resources – not least the human resource.

SO WHAT FOR PERSONNEL?

What is the relevance of this to the personnel function? It is the contention of this book that if personnel professionals and their function are to play the role that is potentially open to them they must move into the strategic arena. To do this requires a good understanding of the whole issue of the formulation and implementation of strategy in today's business environment. This principle applies at a number of levels.

At the corporate level, a personnel perspective can have a key role to play in the development of strategic thinking. As we have seen, it may be important for management to break away from a current mindset. This may be difficult for functional managers with a particular turf to defend. The HR director is better placed than many to help the CEO and the board to break away from accepted norms of thinking and to have an essential part in the determination and implementation of strategy. This is supported by the fact that many of the prime strategic issues involve the human resource anyway.

In Kay's terminology, the people and skills within the business form one of its fundamental distinctive capabilities. It will often be just this dimension of capability which will determine the appropriate strategic direction to be adopted. The Ryder plan was merely a wish list strategy precisely because the company did not possess the human capital to achieve the aspirations espoused by Ryder.

Moreover, as we have seen, these are process issues, and it is very much in the area of process that personnel professionals should bring particular understanding and sensitivity to bear. One of the strongest cards available to them is at least strong influence, and often control, over training and education within the organisation. This provides great opportunities to stimulate a strategic approach to the business. People within an organisation need to have some sense of direction if they are to give of their best. At a basic level, they not only want to know what to do, but why they are doing it! Personnel therefore has a vested interest in bringing about a strategic view of the business.

At the functional level, personnel needs to take a strategic view of its contribution. If the function is to move beyond a reactive administrative service, personnel people must have a grasp of what it means to think in a strategic way. The function needs to ensure that its priorities and capabilities are in 'sync' with, and supportive of, the strategic imperatives of the business as a whole.

Finally, in personal terms, it is increasingly important to take a strategic approach to one's own career development. This is presumably what is implied by the current emphasis on encouraging people to take more responsibility for their own learning, and to develop transferable skills in the interests of long term employability.

There has never been a better opportunity for personnel to develop a strategic approach. The rest of this book is about how to do it.

Key questions

● Does your organisation have a strategic view of the future?

● Do you know what it is?

● Which of the following statements most clearly corresponds to your personal mindset?

— 'To perform at its best, an organisation needs to develop a strategic plan covering a three–five year time frame.'

— 'An organisation needs to be clear about strategic objectives, but in an era of rapid change strategy needs to be extremely flexible.'

— 'Strategy is a jargon word for the aggregation of day to day operational decisions made by skilled managers.'

Notes

1. Tregoe, B and Zimmerman, J *Top Management Strategy*, see Bibliography.
2. Mintzberg, Henry *The Rise and Fall of Strategic Planning*, see Bibliography.
3. Quinn, James B and Mintzberg, Henry *The Strategy Process: Cases*, see Bibliography.
4. Kay, John *Foundations of Corporate Success*, see Bibliography.
5. *Harvard Business Review* (1992) September–October p27.

2
People Provide the Edge

" Future success depends on enabling everyone,
regardless of gender, ethnic background or disability,
to use their abilities to the full. When staff typically
constitute the biggest item in the cost base;
when knowhow and innovation are the stock in trade;
it makes excellent commercial sense to invest in human
assets and to engender a maximum return on that investment " .

Lord Alexander of Weedon QC, chairman,
National Westminster Bank plc

We have arrived at a time when the art and science of management are
undergoing radical transformation. At the heart of this transformation
lies a new realisation of the essential importance of people within any
business. In 1992, the Confederation of British Industry (CBI) set out its
blueprint for the revitalisation of British manufacturing: 'Industry has to
achieve a substantial improvement in performance over several years to
compete internationally on a sustainable basis.'[1] Among company
priorities was included 'to recognise that people are the crucial factor in a
business'.

THE NEW LOOK – FACT OR FAD?

Personnel professionals have learned to be sceptical with regard to the
numerous protestations over the years by company chairmen, in annual
reports and elsewhere, about employees as the 'key assets' of the company. Too often this has been in clear contradiction to actual practice,
typically in terms of the value placed by senior management on training.

However, there are now indications that an increasing number of
boards of directors are beginning to recognise that they will be damaged
if they do not give the human side of their business real priority. Top

class companies – and there are many in the UK, as well as elsewhere – know that having a talented, well trained, and committed workforce is paramount in maintaining a competitive edge in the company's chosen market.

Jack Welch, of General Electric fame, has expressed it in typical fashion:

> I think any company that's trying to play in the 1990s has got to find a way to engage the mind of every single employee. Whether we make our way successfully down this road is something only time will tell – but I'm sure this is the right road.
>
> If you're not thinking all the time about making every person more valuable, you don't have a chance. What's the alternative? Wasted minds? Uninvolved people? A labor force that's angry or bored? That doesn't make sense!
>
> If you've got a better way, show me, I'd love to know what it is.

EXAMPLES

From Royal Mail to Channel Tunnel

In the early 1990s, one of the UK's largest employers embarked on a process of change which they called 'Business Development'. Royal Mail employed some 180,000 staff and handled 60 million items daily. Business Development was intended to supplement previous initiatives, for example on Total Quality, and at its heart was the workforce. New structures were introduced, which were likened by the managing director to an 'inverted pyramid'. At the top were all those – postmen and women – who dealt directly with the customer. All the organisation's other resources were designed to support and service the people who – literally – delivered the goods.

All very well, one might say, for an organisation such as Royal Mail, whose task is so obviously people oriented. In fact, similar examples are proliferating across the whole industrial and commercial spectrum. The recent completion of the Channel Tunnel provides a spectacular example. The book commemorating the opening of the Tunnel rightly celebrates the 'Eleven Formula 1 Moles', the famous tunnelling machines, costing between £8m and £33.5m each. It goes on to state:

> The Channel tunnel project is without doubt a unique showcase of technology, but it also represents a fantastic laboratory of human resources. The tunnel was built by people, and not by machines. Nearly

13,000 engineers and technicians worked together on both sides of the Channel. The popular press in Britain called them 'the Tunnel Tigers'.

The energy of Amoco

A similar principle was enunciated by the CEO of a leading energy company, Amoco Corporation, at a world wide meeting of senior executives in February 1993.[2] He made it clear that people, not technology, will provide the company's competitive edge:

> The critical component of the competitive advantage we need to develop is people. In fact, the single most important task before us is to engage all the talent, all the teamwork, and team spirit, all the energy and drive, all the initiative and all the commitment of everyone in the Amoco family.

This people focus was promulgated throughout the organisation. The business of the most technology driven of its subsidiaries, Amoco Production Company, is exploration and the production of petroleum and natural gas, but it recognised that even in that business 'people provide the edge':

> Superior execution depends on people. To succeed in implementing business strategies, we must first succeed in implementing people and organisational strategies. We must work together. We must help each other to be the best we can. And we must create a climate in which people can excel, because people provide the edge.

Allied Signals

A similar message came through strongly in a recent interview with another senior chief executive, Lawrence Bossidy of American corporation, Allied Signals:[3] 'I am convinced that nothing we do is more important than hiring and developing people. At the end of the day, you bet on people, not on strategies'.

The UK's very own ICI

ICI is another company which has undergone enormous changes in recent years. Much of the way change has been handled stemmed from a view that the best way to improve the business's performance was to improve the performance of the people working in it. ICI's chief executive stated early on in the process, 'The whole process I am outlining is aimed at people'. More formally, a document setting out the group-wide initiative emphasised that 'the future success of the various businesses in ICI depends on developing the talents and performance of its employees'.

From chemicals to motor racing

Kay, in his book quoted in Chapter 1, gives as one of his examples, the case of Cosworth Engineering. The firm is cited as providing a rare example of British commercial success and engineering excellence in one of the world's most competitive environments – motor racing. In the end, Cosworth depends on its people, deploying them in a particular way:

> Important as a complete understanding of technical detail has been to management decision-making, Cosworth is a company with the potential to create its own competition. This is because the company only survives by encouraging talented people to develop and exploit know-how that cannot be exclusively controlled by the company through patenting.

This is an illustration of Kay's main thesis, that a firm's competitive advantage derives from one or other 'distinctive capabilities'. The first of the primary sources of such capability is what the writer calls 'architecture' – a network of relational contracts within or around the firm. And prime among these is the internal architecture created by relationships with and between employees.

In most cases, a characteristic of effective architecture is that it 'does not create extraordinary organizations by collecting extraordinary people. It does so by enabling very ordinary people to perform in extraordinary ways'. (A characteristic borne out incidentally by Belbin's work on effective teams.)

A survey conducted jointly by Price Waterhouse and Henley Management College asked senior executives of firms in the M4 corridor, the so-called 'Golden Triangle', to identify the factors likely to be of most importance to their companies over the next five years. The great majority rated human resources within at least the top five.

SUCCESSFUL TRANSFORMATION

Over the last few years, a number of companies have undertaken major transformation initiatives, to respond to the dramatic change, even threats, facing them. John Kotter, Professor of Leadership at the Harvard Business School, recently produced a list of the steps which his research has shown to be vital to success.[4] These are:

- Establishing a sense of urgency
- Forming a powerful guiding coalition
- Creating a vision
- Communicating a vision
- Empowering others to act on the vision
- Planning for and creating short-term wins
- Consolidating improvements and producing still more change
- Institutionalising new approaches.

These steps are shot through with personnel issues. For example, 'communicating the vision' involves using every vehicle possible to achieve effective communications. 'Planning for and creating short-term wins' requires among other things recognising and rewarding employees involved in the improvements. 'Institutionalising new approaches' has important implications for management development and succession.

The fact is that illustrations of the importance of people to business success abound. One company decided to broadcast the fact on London Underground. An advertisement informed us:

> At Whitbread Inns, we offer our customers the best service possible. Maintaining these high standards and at the same time running a business with a turnover of £3/4m isn't easy, so how do our pub managers manage it? In a word, training, or in three words the best training. Every Whitbread pub manager is backed by one of the finest training programmes in the country. It's a level of training that many other companies can only aspire to. In fact, we've won more national training awards than they've had pub lunches. If you're keen to be trained to run a thriving business, call Whitbread Inns hotline.

Sir Graham Day expressed it in a pithy way during a presentation about his extensive business experience – 'the key is always the people – and the people is always the most difficult'.

THE NEED FOR RADICAL NEW MANAGEMENT

It is not just fashion or fad which has brought people to the top of the corporate agenda, but the fact that radical changes are taking place in the way organisations are managed. This amounts to no more nor less than a managerial revolution. Peter Drucker's latest book *Post-Capitalist Society* describes this as part of a wider canvas. In the emerging society which is already visible in current trends, the dominant feature is no longer physical or financial capital but human capital – or what Drucker calls 'knowledge'.

– AND THE FACTORS BEHIND IT

What are some of the factors which combine to create this new situation?

The rise of individualism and the nature of authority

A characteristic of knowledge workers is that they tend to be individualistic. Drucker's analysis concludes that the emerging society will be full of specialists who cannot be managed in the old way by bosses who know less about the matter in hand than they do. The London Human Resource Group's study on *Winning People* forecasts a demand for 21,000 new jobs in the City of London by 1998. But the makeup of this figure is telling; it predicates 10,000 fewer clerical jobs, but an increase of 30,000 knowledge workers. The trend is clear across the board. In engineering there is a dramatic movement underway transforming the old skilled 'blue collar' elite into specialised technicians.

This situation goes hand in hand with new managerial approaches such as individual contracts of employment, and the opening of channels of communication direct to the workforce, cutting across old collective arrangements. No organisations have suffered more from the move from the collective to the individual than the trade unions.

Part of this trend is the nature of authority in contemporary society. One young school-leaver attending an induction day in her first job responded to the question 'What are you looking for in a job?' with the classic reply 'I don't only want to know what to do, I want to know why I'm doing it'. The days when the manager's job was to tell employees what to do and then constantly check whether they were doing it are over. This 'command and control' role has been replaced by the coach/ enabler model, partly because people's attitudes to authority have changed and they will no longer accept the old approach.

Some attempts to introduce 'empowerment' founder on this point. There is a distinctly paternalistic flavour to the word. The implication is that the process is in the gift of management; those who empower can also disempower if they so decide. The truth is that individuals already have the power – at the very least to withdraw wholehearted effort – and management's task is to engender the environment where this power is aligned with the organisation's objectives.

Bossidy of Allied Signal talks of 'the CEO as coach':[3] The day when you could yell and scream and beat people into good performance is over. Today you have to appeal to them by helping them see how they can get from here to there, by establishing some credibility, and by giving them some reason and some help to get there. Do all those things, and they'll knock down doors.

The new economy

In his book *Global Paradox: The Bigger the World Economy, the More Powerful its Smallest Players*, John Naisbitt points out that America's Fortune 500 companies now account for only 10 per cent of the US economy, down from 20 per cent in 1970. Even the giant companies employ far fewer people than in the recent past: for example IBM – down to around 300,000 from 400,000 in 1985. Digital – 98,000 now as compared to 126,000 in 1989. Moreover they are in competition with minnows in terms of numbers employed; Apple with about 15,000 and Microsoft with 13,000.

A summary of this new emerging economy appeared in *Fortune* magazine in May 1993,[5] setting out 'six trends that will reshape the workplace':

- The average company will become smaller, employing fewer people
- The traditional hierarchical organisation will give way to a variety of forms, foremost being the network of specialists
- Technicians, ranging from computer repairpeople to radiation therapists, will replace manufacturing operatives as the worker elite
- The vertical division of labour will be replaced by a horizontal division
- The paradigm of doing business will start from making a product to providing a service
- Work itself will be redefined: constant learning, more high order thinking, less nine-to-five.

The paradigm shift from making a product to providing a service applies just as much in manufacturing as in service businesses. The drive for quality in manufacturing means in effect building more service into the product.

Drucker emphasises that these trends lead inexorably to 'contracting out'. This enables people to concentrate on what they are good at and qualified for. Directly employed cleaners are low grade and lowly valued employees. Contracted out to a specialist firm, cleaning becomes the prime activity of those concerned and is highly valued by senior executives as the whole raison d'etre of the enterprise.

The impact of technology

Clearly, the development of new technologies is a factor of huge importance in this revolution. In 1993, for the first time more PCs than cars were sold around the world – the information society is already under way. As Naisbitt points out, the shift from the mainframe to the PC is an excellent metaphor for the move from bureaucracy to small autonomous units. Mainframes added computer number crunching power, but did not alter ways of managing. They needed vertical hierarchies and required substantial numbers of employees to run them on-site. The new technology is taking over more and more work that can be routinised, and is less concerned with producing goods than with transmitting information. It provides enormous opportunities to look again at the way we work. The insistent question now is 'can we do this a better way?'

The old technology impacted a company's control systems and procedures, whereas the new is more concerned with market mechanisms – the delivery of service. Tesco places 95 per cent of its orders to suppliers through electronic data exchange. The company has electronic links with over 13,000 suppliers and over 55 per cent of invoices are sent electronically. In a very different industry, Calsonic Exhaust Systems delivers products directly to Nissan's car production line every 30 minutes. The supplier pays a financial penalty for every minute production is held up by late delivery.

Technology knows no boundaries. With information flashing not just between companies but across national frontiers at the press of a button, we are involved in 'globalisation' in a big way. One company that has combined globalisation with 'small is beautiful' is ABB (Asea Brown Boveri), the world's largest power engineering company with annual revenues exceeding $30bn. The group is divided into 1200 companies averaging 200 employees each. According to the chief executive, Percy Barnevik, 'we are not a global business. We are a collection of local businesses with intense global coordination'. Coordination only made possible through technology.

Individuals as consumers

The purpose of management today is to bring together all these elements, of highly specialised workers, service orientation and the use of new technology to win and hold customers. Firms have to be managed so that they are totally customer driven. Giving customers choice is a prime weapon of competition. This principle applies whether we are talking about consumers on the High Street, or 'high tec' manufacturers. One manufacturer of sophisticated industrial automation equipment has developed a computer network, so that clients can check product specifications and make on-line requests for customised modifications.

BT's Annual Report to Shareholders in 1994 commented on the great changes achieved over the previous ten years:

> There are many factors that have contributed to that change – including the availability of funds for investment, technology improvements and above all, the contribution of our people. But perhaps the key difference between BT 1994 and British Telecom 1984 is that we have reorganised ourselves around the fundamental principle of putting the customer first, and have conducted a revolution in the quality of service we offer.

The link between the way people are managed and the new focus on service was summed up in a motto coined by one of the world's leading financial services companies: Staff motivation = Customer retention.

This concept was at the heart of the philosophy of Jan Carlzon, president of the airline SAS, with his famous phrase 'moments of truth'.[6] He wrote:

> Last year, each of our 10 million customers came in contact with approximately five SAS employees, and this contact lasted an average of 15 seconds each time. Thus, SAS is 'created' 50 million times a year, 15 seconds at a time. These 50 million 'moments of truth' are the moments that ultimately determine whether SAS will succeed or fail as a company. If we are truly dedicated to orienting our company toward each customer's individual needs, then we cannot rely on rule books and instructions from distant corporate offices. We have to place responsibility for ideas, decisions, and actions with the people who are SAS during those 15 seconds: ticket agents, flight attendants, baggage handlers and all the other frontline employees.

From soft to hard – the drive to cut costs

Undoubtedly one major reason why the human resource has come to the top of the corporate agenda is cost. As businesses shift increasingly from churning out product to adding a quality service, labour accounts for a higher proportion of costs. Equally, specialist knowledge workers may well command a premium price in the market-place. Under the force of competition, employers naturally look to drive down their cost base and the easiest way to cut costs is to reduce employee numbers. People may be a precious resource; they are also an extremely costly one.

Managing the cost of the human resource is not simply a numbers game. Overall, management must seek to ensure the best return on this costly investment. This objective clearly leads straight into the big issues of productivity and performance, and ultimately into all facets of human resource management.

PEOPLE ARE NOW AT THE HEART OF MANAGEMENT PRACTICE

All these issues – the rise of individualism, the new economy, the impact of technology, globalisation, new consumer demands and the ever increasing cost of the human resource – mean that organisations cannot be managed in the old way. Indeed, perhaps the biggest change of all concerns the role of managers themselves. The *Fortune* article[5] even suggested that the job title of manager is on the way out. The best employers realise that they have to seek out new ways of managing – the remainder will ultimately have to follow suit or go out of business.

A powerful statement about the implications of this for the practice of management and leadership in today's world was made by one of the most effective of contemporary leaders in the world of sport. This was the late Sir John Smith, former chairman of a great football club: 'We are the management team. We talk every day of our lives about players, about how to sustain and improve things. It is a cliché, but a truism, that we are servants of the many who sustain Liverpool FC.'

In practical terms, these developments have led to many new facets of management practice. Experience shows that people are at the heart of these initiatives and the initiatives seem to fail or at least be only half effective if this is not taken properly into account. Examples include:

● mergers and acquisitions
● re-engineering

- productivity
- downsizing
- management of technology.

Mergers and acquisitions

The success of any merger or acquisition is highly dependent on managing cultural differences. How do the respective firms go about their business? What are the social and educational backgrounds of key executives? Does the company to be acquired have a hierarchical or flat structure? Does it recognise trade unions and how does it manage the relationship? What do the compensation and benefits policies signify? For example, are they highly geared to individual or team performance? Who are the role models among the senior group and what seem to be their values?

These and other questions can provide the basis for an audit of human resource management that will provide essential information if the new company is to be successfully integrated.

Once the merger or acquisition is agreed, it has to be managed and again this is critical to success. In their book *Mergers and Acquisitions: The Human Factors*, Cartwright and Cooper list some essential early action. Examples are:

- The handling of the merger announcement sets the tone. Does management take care to inform employees properly, as well as the financial press?
- Employees need to be afforded opportunities to participate in change; management needs to demonstrate an intention to consult.
- communication with employees must be of a high order. It needs to use the language of shared learning and indicate a grasp of those issues which are of high concern to employees.

Templeton's Hubbard and Purcell have conducted considerable research in this area.[7] They note the importance of managing employee expectations during the integration of any acquired business, and confirm many of the same issues as Cartwright and Cooper. An additional point is the need to renegotiate the psychological contract with every new employee. To quote the researchers: 'they aren't mind readers!'

Re-engineering

There is ample evidence that human factors lie at the heart of the success or failure of attempts to re-engineer business processes. A survey by Ernst & Young of 27 companies claiming to adopt process innovation concluded:

> On the subject of successfully implementing process change, 23 of the 27 companies report that the biggest challenge is to convince employees that change is necessary and to obtain their commitment to the programme. In contrast, none of the companies have found that technical problems threaten the success of their programmes – the people dimension is the most difficult factor in process innovation.

This survey was quoted in a *Management Today* report 'Re-engineering: the Critical Success Factors' by David Harvey. The author amplifies the point:

> However compelling a plan to re-engineer a company may look on paper, it becomes reality only when it is accepted and implemented by those who have to operate the new processes. Standing between the ambition and its implementation are the dead weight of custom and practice, vested interests, fears of the unknown, and the corporate culture which underpins the status quo. The more radical the change, the greater the fear and uncertainty, and also the greater the resistance registered by those affected. Given the choice, many will cling to the present, with all its imperfections, in preference to letting go for an unproven prospect of better things to come.
>
> All the companies which have successfully re-engineered their businesses insist that there must be sufficient incentive for people to adopt new working practices and conditions. Further, they must be involved in mapping out the new order and have a chance to air their views, doubts and aspirations. This is the human dimension of re-engineering. Leaving change management to chance is one of the surest ways of courting disaster.

The survey includes a number of case studies, including for example the Xerox Group. Here, one of the challenges was 'to persuade managers and staff to work in more flexible, collaborative and creative ways'. Empowerment was actively promoted by senior managers, while managers generally were encouraged to give as much attention to the personal development of their team as to attaining business results. Performance in the newly structured company was measured on four indicators: customer satisfaction; employee motivation and satisfaction; market share; and return on assets.

Another case quoted was that of Western Provident. The very first priority in starting down the transformation road was to rebuild morale and establish the commitment of staff to the business.

Productivity

Following research into new approaches to productivity among European car engine manufacturers, researchers Frank Mueller of London Business School and John Purcell of Templeton derived what they called the 'productivity improvement wheel'.[8] At the centre of the wheel is productivity improvement, and the spokes are the factors delivering the improvement. On one side of the wheel are technical factors improving machine running time, such as new technology, integration of maintenance, and workflow management techniques. On the other side, and of equal weight, are factors improving teamworking, such as continuous training, employee involvement, and a skill attainment pay system.

The researchers described this as an integrated approach to productivity improvement; the research indicated that some of the elements implemented in isolation were unlikely to prove effective. What mattered was the capacity to think through and act on all the components of the wheel in an integrated way.

Downsizing

The need to control and in many instances to cut costs is another factor in this whole equation. The way this is done has a huge impact on the company's future. It reflects not only on those immediately affected – many of whom will be customers and opinion formers – but on those who remain, on whom the company depends for its future. Writing in *Harvard Business Review* on 'Why Transformation Efforts Fail', John Kotter recognised the issue:

> Gaining understanding and support is tough when downsizing is a part of the vision. For this reason, successful visions usually include new growth possibilities and the commitment to treat fairly anyone who is laid off.

A highly significant example is that of BT. In its 1994 Report to Shareholders, the company met this issue head on.

> Our continued downsizing programme was again successful, and the year saw the departure of a further 13,300 of our people on entirely voluntary redundancy terms. Since 1990, we have reduced the workforce by more

than 80,000 (35%), in a sensitive and controlled manner, while continuing to deliver a world-class service to our customers.

Later, the report responded to questions about cost control:

We know that we need highly motivated people to ensure our customers get the best possible service. However, if we are to become the most efficient telecommunications company in the world, we also know that we must control wage costs. It is a fact that pay within BT is very good by comparison with equivalent salaries in competing organisations.

Reducing employee numbers and limiting pay increases will inevitably have an impact on morale. In order to track such concerns, we periodically survey our employees about a range of issues, from which we derive a programme of action for individual divisions.

The management of technology

Many organisations have found that it is no good pouring millions of pounds into the development of technology unless the human factor is taken fully into the equation. All the lessons of involving people in the implementation of change come into play. Moreover, there is also the particular problem of the relationship between information technology (IT) staff and their internal customers. IT staff have their own professional skills, standards and values which may or may not sit well with those in the organisation at large.

Another issue concerns specifications for IT assignments. Who owns them? Are the customers committed to them? One company was making substantial investments in new IT systems, but the results were never wholly satisfactory. It transpired that managers of departments for whom the project was intended were signing off the initial project specification, without reading them, because they did not understand them. When the project failed to live up to expectations, there were recriminations all round. Relationships deteriorated, to the detriment of future projects.

CONCLUSION

This chapter has explored the nature of the radical transformation in management philosophy and practice which is happening all around us. It amounts to nothing less than a revolution in the making. We have seen that this revolution brings with it a new focus on people as the key asset of a business. This clearly has profound implications for those of us in personnel.

Yet in the next chapter, we will see that this transformation is only half complete. The issue for personnel professionals is the extent to which they will succeed in taking a major role in the steps still to come.

Key questions

● What are the most important people issues for your organisation?

● What are the most important ways in which people contribute to the ultimate success of your organisation?

● Does the top management team recognise the vital importance of people to their business?

Notes

1. CBI (1992) *Making it in Britain.*
2. Blessing/White (1994) *Update* Vol 7 No 1.
3. Tichy, Noel M and Cheran, Ram (1995) 'The CEO as Coach – an Interview with Allied Signal's Lawrence A Bossidy' *Harvard Business Review* March–April pp70–8.
4. Kotter, John (1995) 'Leading Change – Why Transformation Efforts Fail' *Harvard Business Review* March–April pp59–67.
5. *Fortune* (1993) May pp39–52.
6. Jan Carlzon, president SAS, *Moments of Truth – New Strategies for Today's Customer-Driven Economy*, see Bibliography.
7. Research funded by the Leverhulme Trust and conducted by Nancy Hubbard and John Purcell of Templeton College Oxford on the human resource implications of mergers and acquisitions.
8. Mueller, Frank and Purcell, John (1992) 'The Drive for Higher Productivity' *Personnel Management* May pp29–32.

3
Personnel at the Crossroads

"Why is the Personnel profession not held in higher regard?
It's because, too often, we've been seen as the department
that likes to say no, rather than as the enabler of change.
We must show that we have moved on from being industrial
relations gunfighters, and are now more about developing
people and organisations for competitive success".
Michael Bett, President, Institute of Personnel and Development.

With people apparently firmly established at the top of the corporate agenda, the personnel function should be riding high. At last, it looks as if managers might actually believe what many have been saying for a long time – that people are the key! Yet, far from basking in the limelight of success, in an uncomfortably large number of boardrooms the personnel profession seems to be held in less esteem than ever. Personnel departments have been slashed and in many cases removed altogether. There is a real danger that the function will be marginalised.

THE FAILURES OF PEOPLE MANAGEMENT

At the same time, it can hardly be said that generally speaking people management is being handled with consummate skill. The Henley/Price Waterhouse survey (see Chapter 2) may have indicated that people issues were considered among the most important factors for business success among a high proportion of senior executives in the Thames Valley/M4 corridor. Yet the same survey reveals that only 39 per cent of company executives felt they had a clearly defined human resource strategy. Research on employers' labour policies conducted for the Department of Employment by Glasgow University and reported in *Employment Gazette* did not reveal a single instance of a written statement of HR strategy.[1]

The London Human Resource Group's study *Winning People* concluded that there was a long way to go before the standard of people management within the City of London could be considered as anywhere near satisfactory. Yet it needs to be world class if the City is to retain its preeminence on a world scale. One corporate affairs director was scathing in his criticism:

> We had business school gurus all over the place. They and we forgot to ask the most basic question – why would staff want to be empowered in a climate of exponential change? But more than that, we forgot to ask 'what's in it for the staff?' Our workforce has been nearly halved, and we are nowhere near achieving our business objectives. Our macho style of senior management has overlooked many common sense questions. We shall continue to pay the price until the last of them switches off the light and leaves.

The final section of *Winning People* is headed rather plaintively 'Preparing for Uncertainty: Personnel, where are you?'. It cites the two central messages from a recent Harvard study 'Beyond the Hype':

- It is easy to wax lyrical about new management practices for a new age
- The rhetoric of management has increased sharply in change programmes, but its practices have stayed very much the same.

Studies of quality initiatives show that a high proportion fail. Such failure is more often than not attributable to the fact that the human element involved has not been taken properly into account. The 1993 IPM study of quality management[2] indicated a strong link between employee dissatisfaction and problems with successful implementation.

The Institute of Work Psychology at the University of Sheffield is currently conducting a study of corporate performance in the UK manufacturing sector. One hundred and fifteen UK manufacturing companies are involved in the project, the aim of which is to identify how manufacturing firms in the UK can be most effective, in terms of both economic performance and employee well-being. Initial findings make somewhat depressing reading:

> Whilst there is evidence of much managerial effort, views from the shop floor suggest there is a large gap between espoused practices and reality. Human Resource Management is generally neglected in these manufacturing firms. Forty percent of the sample had no personnel staff, whilst

two-thirds had no personnel or HRM strategy. Almost half had no training strategy, despite widespread attempts to train in areas such as quality. Training needs analysis was also poor or absent in over half the companies.

Job variety, richness and responsibility remain very limited for many shop floor workers, with most shop floor jobs being repetitive and monotonous. Two-thirds of firms had no deliberate policy of job rotation. Equal opportunities is not generally perceived an important issue, with two-thirds of firms having no stated policy on the subject. Participation, open communications and autonomy are hidden in the landscape of most manufacturing companies.

The research company MORI has been regularly monitoring employee attitudes over a number of years across a wide spectrum of organisations. Latest findings show widespread feelings of alienation of employees from their companies.

Problems with change

Many of the critical change processes undertaken by organisations have run into difficulties. The problems of many of the prestigious institutions who rushed into merger mode following the City's Big Bang are well documented. Indeed, several studies show that over half of all mergers and acquisitions fail to achieve their original objectives and some have led to the loss of as many as 75 per cent of the managerial team.

Purcell and Ahlstrand's book *Human Resource Management in the Multi-Divisional Company* is critical of the lack of human resource planning in mergers:[3]

> The personnel and human resource implications of strategic management are often not considered adequately. We have been surprised to find, in our research, relatively few examples of serious human resource planning linked to strategic management. Yet personnel type problems often emerge after a new company has been acquired or a major capital or divestment decision taken. These often relate to such issues as the failure to identify the drain on management resources in the parent company; the problem of integrating different cultures and practices; and thorny industrial relations issues such as pay parity or union recognition.

In the 1980s, certain financial institutions became concerned that estate agents could move to become distributors of their retail products, such as mortgages and insurance. Their response was to go on the acquisition trail, and many estate agents were bought up. In many cases, the outcome was a substantial loss and some have withdrawn from that market. The problems were primarily due to a lack of the right kind of management skills on the part of the acquirers, who had focused on financial factors, while paying insufficient heed to human ones.

Meanwhile, personnel often seems powerless, a hapless bystander. A study by Hegarty and Hoffman published in the journal *Long Range Planning*, compared the influence of various functions on strategic decision making.[4]

On a scale of 0 to 5, the managing director had a score of 3.8, and the finance function 2.8. Marketing scored 3.2. Personnel scored less than 2, indicating almost no influence. Admittedly this study is somewhat old in the tooth, being published in 1987, but who would be brave enough to say that the picture has hugely changed since then in the great generality of organisations?

We seem therefore to be faced with the following combination of factors:

● The way people are managed is an increasingly critical factor.
● There seems to be fairly widespread recognition of this.
● Practice is often far removed from what is needed.
● The personnel function is not making the impact it should.

In this chapter, we analyse the reasons for this state of affairs and consider the way forward.

OLD-STYLE PERSONNEL

Old-style personnel reached its peak in the 1970s. Personnel management had largely shaken off its 'welfare' image, and had found its own place in the sun. Among other things, it had developed a particular expertise, and hence power base, in industrial relations. In an era of substantial union strength in the workplace, line managers were understandably reluctant to stick their necks out and take independent decisions, for fear of upsetting a delicate apple cart. A far safer policy was to consult with personnel. A high premium was placed by management on negotiating skills, and an ability to see the way through often arcane union agreements.

Personnel managers saw it as their business to establish good working relationships with shop stewards and union officials. This appealed to the officials concerned who often saw personnel as more powerful than in reality it was. Indeed, in many cases a community of interest often developed, rather like the relationship between barristers acting for plaintiff and defendant. Personnel may have officially bemoaned the increasing influence of shop stewards, as power shifted from national union officials to the shop floor, but it was not all bad news. Many a career was based on the ability to pull the fat out of the fire by way of a deal in a smoke filled room.

It was perhaps not surprising that the personnel profession aligned itself with the 'wets' in the intense debates about trade union legislation in the early 1980s. Many sincerely felt that the attack on trade union power was ill conceived, but it was equally an attack on the personnel function's vested interest.

Personnel and corporatism

If such comments seem harsh, it may be said in mitigation that the role adopted by personnel was essentially a reaction to the social, economic and political trends of the day, and indeed to the way industry was organised. Until the 1980s, government policy of whatever colour was concerned to establish a corporate framework for directing commercial affairs. It was perceived to be the natural role of lawmakers to ensure that the rights and security of workers was protected. This extended not only to matters such as health and safety and unfair breaches of contract, but to issues of union membership, collective bargaining and the right to strike.

Since the mid-'60s, legislation had played an ever more intrusive part in the workplace. An important role for personnel managers evolved from legislation against unfair dismissal. Many managers assumed from this that they no longer had the right to dismiss an employee under virtually any circumstances and turned increasingly to personnel for help in dealing with issues of poor performance and misbehaviour. The law set up processes for determining problems of union recognition and at one stage collective agreements were assumed to be legally binding unless the agreement stated otherwise.

Such centralised control was not reserved solely for industrial relations. Training was another vexed area where government believed that employers would do too little too late unless coerced by legislative sticks and carrots. Again, personnel was in the forefront of ensuring that their employer gained maximum return from the levy/grant system imposed by the Industrial Training Act.

Personnel's influence was equally enhanced by government's continuing efforts to tackle an inflation ridden economy by means of a variety of statutory pay policies. Beating the latest pay freeze or norm became a prime concern for the successful personnel manager, and remuneration experts, both within organisations and as consultants, devised ever more sophisticated approaches to pay structures.

All these influences provided great opportunities for personnel professionals to establish an influential role within organisations. In particular, major corporations set up large personnel departments at the centre to manage systems, to monitor policy and to provide expertise. Not surprisingly, personnel responded to these challenges and geared itself up accordingly.

Personnel and Taylorism

However, such external factors were not the only influences moulding the personnel function. It was also responding to the way work itself was structured within organisations. A study carried out in the Netherlands as part of a research programme on technology, work and organisation perceived that personnel management was rooted in 'Tayloristic' concepts of production methods.[5]

> Looking back in time, it has to be concluded that the personnel function developed out of the classic organisation paradigms of scientific management.

In the classic Tayloristic organisation, work was divided into separate control tasks, each under a specific supervisor. This in turn led to the establishment of staff employees concerned with recruitment and selection, reward and so on. The study points out that:

> ... since World War 2, all these staff functions of clerks, bosses, and supervisors have evolved into organisational disciplines and professions, with their own training facilities, standards, professional associations and magazines. In this way, we can recognise the routing clerk in materials management, the inspector in quality assurance, and the repair boss in maintenance. The primary function of these disciplines is sustaining and perfecting the Tayloristic production system.

Personnel responded to this situation. The system lent itself to bureaucratic approaches to all the facets of personnel management. So, for example, there has been a heavy emphasis on job descriptions. These tend to focus on the differences between the various jobs and functions of an organisation, rather than facilitating their interdependence. Training needs analysis stemmed from the same basis of clearly defined jobs and a view that performance depended on the worker being equipped with skills and knowledge specific to that function.

In the same way, it became important to be able to compare tasks for pay purposes, leading naturally to often elaborate methods of job evaluation. The structure lent itself to well defined career paths, and, naturally, hierarchy. Personnel advocated properly ordered succession planning.

Industrial relations itself flows from this state of affairs. The separation of tasks and groups was reflected in multi-unionism, and many disputes stemmed from the need to maintain equitable 'differentials'.

Dealing with breakdowns

With its concern for people, personnel was in a good position to identify the shortcomings of the system. There were for example constant breakdowns in communications between departments, so personnel stepped in to devise systematic solutions to the issue. The discipline of 'organisational development' could be seen as a quasi-scientific attempt to bridge the yawning gap between departments which so often be-devilled companies, and personnel often played an important role by facilitating team building.

The Dutch study[5] also points out that personnel management is a separate function in itself within the bureaucracy. The authors conclude that this has consequences for the way personnel policy is formulated and is a major cause of the difficulty of integrating personnel into business development as a whole. A strictly functional approach is not conducive to the holistic approach demanded by today's conditions.

It is not merely chance that this important phase of personnel management coincided with some of the more formalised approaches to strategy, which we discussed in Chapter 1. It was part and parcel of an attempt to manage organisations according to highly controlled, scientific principles and personnel was able to lend considerable expertise to the enterprise.

The function disadvantaged

If both external factors and the dynamics of the way production was organised combined to give an important role to personnel, they also disadvantaged the function in three important ways. First, they left personnel as essentially a control mechanism – hence with the reputation of being the department that always says no. As van Sluijs puts it:

> ... the Personnel function is left with making manageable the 'unreliable' factor of human labour and with softening the blow by means of, for example, work group consultation, job design, work structuring, and appraisal interviews. This mode of operating can be characterised as treatment of the symptoms.

This left personnel as a 'necessary evil'. Important to the business – yes – but really at its heart – no.

Secondly, the profession was encouraged to concentrate on developing specialised functions. The education and training of personnel professionals placed much emphasis on specialised techniques and many built their career around one or other of the various different areas of personnel – IR, remuneration and benefits, training, and so on. The function has evolved into these discrete fields, which in a bureaucracy can take on a life of their own. All this was quite natural, because this was where the demand was, but functionaries don't lead businesses.

Thirdly, personnel professionals were tempted to seek their security in their industrial relations or other expertise. This is fine so long as the expertise is in demand, but, as we now know, may become a liability as the world changes. Day to day industrial relations have passed irrevocably to line management, and some personnel managers are left high and dry.

The limits of the functional organisation

The limited nature of functional management is a theme common to all the case studies described in Harvey's book on re-engineering (see Bibliography – Chapter 2). In fact, Harvey calls process management 'the death knell for functional management'. The Baxi Partnership for example saw functional organisation as more disabling than enabling. The chief executive of Xerox was quoted as saying:

> ... for decades, we have run the organisation as a large functional machine, which is governed by decisions made at the centre. We've created a system that is complex and which prevents people from taking responsibility. We have overburdened the top of the organisation with the requirements to make a lot of decisions that it is not well equipped to make.

At the beginning of the decade, IBM
Towers Perrin to undertake a worldwide human.
they entitled, somewhat dramatically, *Priorities for Comp*
– A 21st Century Vision. They sought information from CEOs
line executives, HR executives, university faculty and consultants in
countries. Of respondents, 29 per cent were from Europe, of which 9
per cent were from the UK. The US represented 40 per cent.
Approximately 3000 completed questionnaires were returned. One
section of the questionnaire concerned the organisation of the personnel
department. Respondents were asked to choose between two models
for the future:

- organised functionally around areas such as benefits, recruiting and
  training
- organised flexibly around the work to be done, issues and projects.

The response indicated almost a complete reversal over time. Only 15
per cent reported flexible organisations at the time of response, but 74
per cent preferred them for the year 2000.

Personnel under pressure

This background goes some way to explaining why many personnel
people have found it difficult to respond to the new pressures put on
them. They have been caught on the one hand by new approaches which
they are ill equipped to handle, and on the other by the tremendous
economic and competitive squeeze on business. The situation has
undoubtedly put many personnel professionals under pressure to prove
their worth.

There are other ways in which personnel specialists have been their
own worst enemy or are experiencing considerable difficulty. These
include:

- A failure to 'sell' the function. Often, personnel staff do a good job
  and assume that their line colleagues appreciate this. Unfortunately,
  you make that assumption at your peril. Personnel people are not
  always natural salespeople, and the concept of proactive internal PR
  does not sit comfortably with them.
- Line managers tend to see personnel work as essentially common
  sense – until they try it for themselves! We do not articulate effectively enough that personnel is based on sophisticated skills,

knowledge and experience. It is not a 'low tec' activity, which anyone with time to spare could perform, but is often perceived as such.

● Life in the typical personnel department is hectic with demands coming in virtually non-stop. Personnel staff can get bogged down with the immediate day to day pressures, especially when the function's resources are being cut to the bone.

PERSONNEL FACING A NEW AGENDA

It is clear from what has been touched on already in this book that the personnel function faces a radically new agenda. This may be an exciting or a daunting prospect, but it is a reality. Many professionals are simply not equipped to tackle this. We deal with the agenda in detail in chapter 7, but the principles are as follows:

● All personnel activity must be linked closely to business needs and to serve the customer – and be seen to do so.
● The personnel function must be managed holistically. Boundaries between aspects of the function must be subject to teamwork and the closest possible professional cooperation.
● The function must make a major contribution to the task of managing the tensions and contradictions between short term commercial pressures and vital long term development.
● Personnel people must be alive to the fact that priorities are changing.

This last point was graphically illustrated by the results of the work carried out by the Personnel Standards Lead Body.[6] Their functional survey covering almost 1000 senior personnel practitioners identified areas of importance to organisational success and asked questions about the level of competence in those areas. The results were clear – the function performed best in its traditional areas of recruitment, pay and benefits and grievance handling. It performed least well in the 'new' areas, such as promoting communication, performance management processes and enhancing individual capabilities.

PERSONNEL'S ROLE IN THE EMERGING SCENARIO

Facing up to these challenges in a strategic way is the theme of this book and in subsequent chapters we will be looking at each aspect in some detail. However, before moving on to more detailed considerations, we need to give thought to the overall role of personnel. Personnel is moving to a different relationship with line management – what should be its role in the emerging scenario?

Devolution to the line

One crucial trend is the devolution of personnel issues to line management. We have already referred to this in terms of industrial relations. The nature of industrial relations has changed with the reduction of trade union power. In 1984 73 per cent of all workplaces of 25 or more employees had union members; by 1990 this had reduced to 64 per cent. In 1984 66 per cent of employers with 25 or more employees recognised unions; by 1990 the figure was 53 per cent. The scope of collective bargaining has been substantially diminished. This sea change has led to the collapse of personnel's traditional power base. It has handed over responsibility to the line, sometimes voluntarily – or sometimes the line has simply seized the initiative willy-nilly.

The standards developed for vocational qualification purposes by the Management Charter Initiative illustrate the move towards managerial devolution. A function labelled 'manage people' accounts for more than 40 per cent of the units of managerial competence that must be demonstrated by line managers seeking diploma level status. A 1992 MORI survey of 110 personnel professionals from major firms confirmed the trend. The transfer of certain HR responsibilities to line managers was noted by 69 per cent.

As a result, line managers have moved far more into the driving seat. A key finding of the Mueller/Purcell research on productivity[7] was that line managers not only took direct responsibility for managing change, but they were the ones most active in getting things started, the ones most impatient with the status quo. A headline in *Personnel Management* in December 1993 told its own story: 'Personnel opts out of recruitment'. Although this referred to one particular company, there is no doubt that line management is increasingly taking operational decisions that in the past were, rightly or wrongly, handled by personnel specialists.

The former Institute of Personnel Management (IPM) embarked on a project entitled *Managing People – The Changing Frontiers*. A paper produced as part of this exercise[8] stated quite categorically that:

... although the division of responsibility for people management has varied in the past, more recently the balance has been shifting. Line managers are now more fully responsible for the management of performance and they are being encouraged by personnel managers to take a more active part in the recruitment, assessment, reward and development of people. One view of the future is that with the availability of more sophisticated computer software packages, line managers will in due course assume responsibility for most of the routine personnel systems.

One view is that this devolution is a positive development, leaving personnel free to concentrate on more strategic matters. It supports the fact that personnel must be prepared to 'let go' of matters which are clearly a line responsibility. There has always been the danger that personnel would usurp the line responsibility to manage people effectively and, with the best of intentions, this has happened in many organisations over the years. In a firm recruiting a personnel officer for the first time, there was always the risk that managers would greet the new arrival with sighs of relief, on the basis that they would no longer have to deal with all those troublesome people issues and could concentrate on the really important matters like getting new business. We now have an opportunity to regain the right balance.

However, there is another side. In the commentary on its 1992 survey, MORI strikes a cautionary note.[9] Are line managers being equipped to take on these new HR responsibilities? According to the survey results:

... many organisations could be in danger of handing over responsibility for their workforce into hands which may be unprepared, solely because devolution and empowerment have become management 'dogma' without monitoring or process.

Personnel as internal consultant

Devolution is often linked with the concept of personnel as internal consultant and this seems to provide an increasingly popular way forward. It leaves the line free to take operational decisions, and avoids accusations of bureaucracy. However, if this is all there is to personnel, the concept is seriously flawed. It goes so far in the direction of devolution that it leaves personnel with no power base at all. It encourages management to cut the function to a bare minimum and outsource the remainder. This may appeal to the finance director, but hardly appeals to those of us who are arguing for a genuinely strategic contribution from personnel.

If personnel is to have a future, it is not enough simply to hand over responsibility and authority to line management. So what other more sophisticated models are available?

OTHER MODELS

For the personnel manager seeking to move towards a more strategic approach, terms taken from the construction industry provide a useful mental model to chart progress towards the strategic goal (see Table 3.1)[10].

The local government model

The evolution of personnel activity in local government has led to a combination of 'architect' and 'contracts manager'. A small unit at the centre provides core strategic decisions and direction and adds value through a quality assurance role. Operational departments deploy separate 'provider' units; these work on an internal consultancy basis, but at least have a firm contract behind them and the professional

Table 3.1   *The construction industry model*

Clerk of works	Contracts manager	Architect
Little discretion	Some discretion, with limits	High discretion
Short-term planning horizon	Medium term planning horizon	Long term planning horizon
Gives services to junior line managers	Gives service plus advice to middle management	Acts as consultant to senior managers
Follows routines	Provides knowledge of systems and IR practice	Conceptualises/inventive, creative problem solver. Changes routines/systems as necessary
Looks for leadership from fellow managers	Follows systems and modifies to some extent. Gives leadership within existing structures	Copes rapidly with change and leads/ participates with top management team

Source: Tyson and Fell

support of a strategic centre. Central personnel specifies, supervises and monitors the contracts with these provider units.

The central role in multi-divisional operations

Purcell and Ahlstrand[3] are clear about the dangers of an overblown systems-oriented central Personnel function. Purcell argues in favour of a new style streamlined corporate function with a new more dynamic role, and identifies nine possible activities:

- Corporate culture and communications
- Essential policy formulation and monitoring
- Human resource contribution to strategic planning
- 'Cabinet office' services
- Senior management development and career planning
- External advocacy (eg to Whitehall and Brussels)
- Information coordination
- Internal consultancy and mediation services
- Personnel services for small units.

The 'power/integration' matrix

Shipton and McCauley of the Sheffield Business School offer a matrix with four models, where the distinguishing features are the extent to which each model exercises power and/or is integrated into the organisation.[11] This is set out in Figure 3.1.

The business manager model has recently received considerable endorsement from the Personnel Standards Lead Body.[12] It is implicit in its statement of the key purpose of personnel: 'to enable management to enhance the individual and collective contributions of people to the short and long term success of the enterprise'. Its Advisory Forum affirmed that 'Personnel Directors have to behave as general managers with personnel specialisms rather than as personnel people with general management tendencies'.

The administrator is typified by a central personnel department handling systems and procedures, while the organisational development model could also be described as the change agent. Shipton and McCauley point out that such a role may be important where personnel is required to challenge the status quo. This is more difficult if the agent is too fully integrated in the existing organisation.

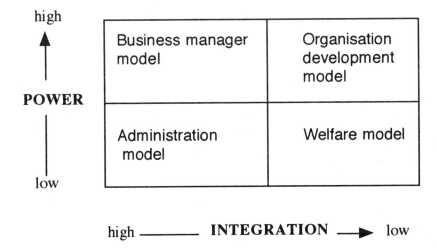

Source: Shipton and McCauley 1993

Figure 3.1 *The power/integration matrix*

Getting the mix right

As always with such models, the best solution is usually a mixture of styles and the more astute personnel practitioners will be good judges of the right approach in any given situation. For example, the business manager model can be taken too far, leading to a 'lean and mean' function good at wielding a hatchet to cut costs, but out of touch with people. It may win corporate friends in the short term, but do a disservice to the organisation in the end. It may ultimately sacrifice people's trust, and the subsequent loss of commitment could be decisive.

On the other hand, as we note elsewhere in this book, the somewhat derided welfare model may be due for something of a comeback, albeit 1990s style.

THE BUSINESS PARTNERSHIP MODEL

The heading of this chapter describes personnel as being 'at the cross-roads'. For a broad vision of the most fruitful direction for the future, we turn to the insights offered by the IBM/Towers Perrin study *Priorities for Competitive Advantage* (see below). One of the strengths of this work was the involvement not only of personnel professionals but also of senior line executives. The questionnaire asked respondents to select and rank 5 items from a list of 17 environmental factors affecting human resource management. Some of these were business and economic factors, such as increased competition or focus on customer satisfaction. Others were 'soft' or people issues such as changing employee values or new skill requirements. The response showed an equal appreciation of both kinds of factors by both line and HR respondents. To quote the commentary on this finding: 'in this shared understanding of the external environment lies a basis for partnerships between line and HR executives to attain business goals'. A similar consensus emerged on questions regarding HR goals.

The study also probed the question of devolution to the line. Here again, a clear consensus emerged between line and HR respondents; both foresaw a strong move towards a shared responsibility for strategy formulation and for the management of HR programmes:

> The impact of the HR department can only be maximised through stronger linkages to business strategy and needs. This will come about through business partnerships between line and HR managers and the sharing of responsibilities that is implicit in any partnership.

One of the enduring features of any lasting partnership is mutual respect. This is too often missing in the relationship between personnel and the line. Line managers, particularly senior managers, often underestimate the skills and expertise offered by their personnel colleagues and the demanding nature of their role. It is easy to make personnel the scapegoat for the organisation's problems. Personnel on the other hand may withdraw into a siege mentality and lose the opportunity to provide a really supportive service.

A straightforward and helpful way of seeing the relationships involved is provided by this checklist of the various hats worn by participants in a change process:

- *Advocate* – the person or function stimulating action by putting forward ideas, persuading and influencing. Clearly an important and legitimate role for personnel.
- *Sponsor* – the person or function with the final say-so; once the decision is made to move ahead, the sponsor gives backing and weight to the action required. This is a line role. Confusion and conflict arises where personnel puts themselves in the sponsor role, or is manoeuvred into it.
- *Agent* – the person or function responsible for making it happen. In

HR matters, the normal personnel role, albeit on occasions as part of a task force or working party.

● *Client* – those for whose benefit the process is intended, or who are subject to it.

Retaining a clear understanding of these roles helps to establish a healthy and effective partnership.

The closing comments of the IBM/Towers Perrin study are worth quoting as a conclusion to this chapter:

> The companies that gain competitive advantage from existing or yet-to-be-discovered human resource initiatives will be those that successfully forge business partnerships between HR and line management to integrate HR capabilities with business needs.

Key questions

● What were the most important aspects of this chapter for you?

● What are the implications for the personnel function?

● What action is open to you to start to develop a strategic HR partnership?

Notes

1. Hunter and Mainnes (1994) 'Employers and labour flexibility: the evidence from case studies' *Employment Gazette* June.
2. Institute of Personnel Management (1993) *Quality – People Management Matters*, IPM, London.
3. Purcell, John and Ahlstrand, Bruce *Human Resource Management in the Multi-Divisional Company*, see Bibliography.
4. Hegarty and Hoffman (1987) 'Who Influences Strategic Decisions?' *Long Range Planning* Vol 20 No 2 p78.
5. van Sluijs, Ed, van Assen, Albert and Friso J, den Hertog (1991) 'Personnel Management and Organizational Change: A Sociotechnical Perspective' *European Work and Organizational Psychologist 1* (1).
6. Personnel Standards Lead Body (1994) *Functional Survey*.
7. Mueller, Frank and Purcell, John (1992) 'The Drive for Higher Productivity' *Personnel Management* May pp29–32.
8. *Managing People – The Changing Frontiers* IPM Consultative Document.
9. Walker, Susan, Managing Director MORI HR Research (1992) 'Empowerment – Where HR Has to Draw the Line' *Human Resources Management* Summer.

10.   Tyson and Fell (1986) *Evaluating the Personnel Function* p23.
11.   Model first appeared in the *Human Resource Management Journal*, Vol 4, No 1 (Personnel Publications Ltd) and is reproduced here by kind permission of the authors, John Shipton and John McCauley of Sheffield Business School.
12.   Personnel Standards Lead Body (1993) *A Perspective on Personnel.*

Part Two

At the Heart of the Debate

Before turning to any plan of action, we need to think through, and be clear about, two matters which lie at the heart of any worthwhile strategy.

First and foremost, there are our customers. All business today needs to be customer driven, and this applies equally to our business as personnel professionals. Initially, we are concerned with internal customers, who they are and how we can best serve them. However, this leads on to an even more important debate: what role do we have in serving the real outside customers who ultimately pay our wages? Here personnel has the opportunity to add value in a number of ways, and to form a strategic alliance with those dealing directly with the external customers, such as sales and marketing people.

The other underlying issue is the question of values. All organisations have values, whether written down or not, and these values have an enormous influence on the way things are done. There is considerable evidence that a company's values may be a determining factor in its long term survival. Personnel policies, processes and practices reflect and reinforce the value system, but do the current values support the organisation's future strategic needs?

What of the personal values of employees? In the past, management expected their employees to leave their own values outside the factory gate or the office or shop door. Is this attitude sustainable today? To what extent do employees' values tune in with the organisation's objectives? Is this question of concern to management in general and personnel in particular?

Personnel practitioners who focus effectively on serving the customer, and help to develop an appropriate set of values within their organisation, are already well on the way to making a genuinely strategic contribution.

4

Personnel and Customers

"He profits most who serves best"
Motto for International Rotary

Like all other functions – and indeed all businesses – personnel exists to serve its customers. The point of departure for all strategic considerations is to bring this prime issue sharply into focus. At first sight, the customers concerned are internal. Dealing with the external customer, what has been called the 'final' customer, is usually seen as a matter for departments such as marketing and sales, whereas personnel is an internal function, serving other departments within the organisation.

In fact, this view is far too limiting and has to be challenged. What if personnel was clearly seen as having a major impact on relations with real customers, those who pay the bills? Such a concept immediately brings the function into a new and more positive light and helps to demonstrate its real contribution to the bottom line.

It is my contention that the personnel function has a major role to play in helping to create the 'customer driven company'. Indeed, it could be said that it has a duty to do so, that this is now among its prime tasks. An alliance with marketing looks an attractive proposition, working as a respected partner in the team which is responsible for winning market share, broadening the customer base and increasing quality business.

SERVING INTERNAL CUSTOMERS

Nevertheless, providing an effective service to its immediate customers within the organisation, and being seen to do so, is essential if the function is to retain credibility. So we need to look at that issue first. And the very first step is to clarify the question – who are our customers?

Many personnel people would assume that they are primarily serving 'line management'; in other words, those junior and middle managers who are their peers and with whom they work most closely. Certainly this group normally shares this assumption and shapes their expectations accordingly. There is much satisfaction for the personnel officer who helps to resolve a tricky 'problem employee' issue or who is able to clarify the practical ramifications of the latest piece of legislation in a positive way.

Ask the average line manager what problems tend to keep him or her awake at night and for the most part these will be people problems. Somehow the technical problems are more susceptible to rational solution – if only people did not get in the way. In this sense, personnel has opportunities to impact favourably in terms of day to day management . This is immediate customer service and at its best personnel can create 'delighted' customers.

Yet top management may see things somewhat differently. Helping line managers is all very well but is hardly strategic. It may be an expensive way to get managers doing properly what they should be doing anyway. The function reports to senior management at one level or another. What results are they looking for ? Are they perhaps not the real customer?

This immediately gives a different sense of the function's priorities and a different perspective as to its prime role. Senior and top management will have agendas which may be a long way from the day to day concerns of the average line manager. Many of the roles for the corporate personnel department listed in the last chapter are obviously designed with senior management needs in mind. These may in fact conflict with the immediate interests of middle management. Pushing through process changes will often require uncomfortable changes at that middle level. The extreme but not uncommon case is 'de-layering', leaving personnel with the uncomfortable task of putting those they regarded hitherto as their customers, out of a job.

Employees as customers

In considering personnel's customers, we need to put yet another group into the arena – employees themselves. This is of course where personnel came from, its roots being in the welfare of those employed by the business. This has become a deeply unfashionable view of the function and most of those who regard themselves as personnel professionals shudder at the very idea!

Nevertheless, there is considerable evidence that an increasing amount of time within personnel departments is being devoted to employee counselling. Issues such as helping employees come to terms with the fact that their job is no longer for life are actually high on the agenda.

Many young people coming into personnel are moved by the concept of working with people; again, an idea which tends to be discouraged by their 'elders and betters'. Yet, as employers reconsider the source of their competitive advantage, the concept begins to look less out of date. Perhaps this is a case, not so much of an idea whose time has come, but rather of one coming around for the second time, albeit in a rather different form. We shall return to this theme in due course.

Differing expectations of customer groups

So the problem for personnel is that these groups of potential customers have differing expectations, some of them conflicting. The BT Annual Report for 1994 gave a graphic illustration of such conflicting demands. The report thanks staff in the traditional way and emphasises the need for continuing commitment. At the same time, it makes clear that there will be ongoing downsizing. This pill is sugared by the fact that the downsizing will be voluntary but implicit is the divergence between those who will have a future in the organisation and those who won't. There are innumerable situations of this kind where the major task of personnel is to reconcile conflicting needs.

This issue was addressed by the IBM/Towers Perrin study (see pages 57–9). Respondents were asked whether personnel should represent the views and concerns of employees or of senior management. In response there was substantially more support for personnel representing the views and concerns of senior management than of employees. However, the most frequent response was that personnel should maintain a neutral or balanced view of the concerns of both groups. Moreover, it was forecast that this approach would become more widespread in the future than it is currently.

Whoever the customer, great problems can arise for personnel if it allows itself to take on an inappropriate role. In one company, management had apparently decided that performance appraisal was an important ingredient in the drive for improved performance. With substantial professional help from the personnel team, they got a programme off the ground, to the extent that employees saw the value to themselves and became highly committed to the process. At that point, management's enthusiasm began to wane; perhaps the initiative had after all been flavour of the month. Supervisors became vociferous that appraisals should be conducted at all levels and voiced their concern to the personnel manager. However, he was unable to re-enthuse his senior line colleagues. Whereupon personnel became the scapegoat for the failure of the programme. In effect, personnel had become in the eyes of their middle management clients the 'sponsor' of the initiative, rather than the 'advocate' and 'agent'.

Saying no to customers

Another kind of problem can occur, in so far as personnel seeing itself as the 'guardian' of policies, or values of the company. Again, conflict may well arise between different groups of internal customers. Senior management may reasonably expect personnel to play this role – indeed I would argue that this is often an important strategic contribution. Yet this means that when a line manager – one of personnel's customers – wishes to adopt a line that is against company policy for short term reasons, personnel will have to stand up and say 'no'.

If personnel has a reputation of being the department that says 'no', it is middle line management which will most often make that accusation. Far from feeling that they receive valuable help from personnel in doing their job, they can often perceive it as a hurdle to be got round, as an obstacle to pragmatic action.

It is also a sad fact of life that employees are often extremely critical of personnel. Unfortunately, we have to face the fact that some of this criticism is justified. The cry is 'we never see personnel', 'personnel did nothing to help us' or 'personnel is more interested in its systems than in people – what is it there for?' Such complaints may reflect the function's failure to see employees as a critical part of their client constituency. On the other hand, they may arise because of conflicting demands from other, more powerful customers. It is all too easy for personnel to become the scapegoat for management's shortcomings.

The obvious conclusion is the continuing need to evaluate priorities. Particularly with limited resources, personnel can't please all the people all the time. In fact, personnel staff sometimes feel that they can't please any of the people at any time!

I have identified here one of the most difficult challenges for any personnel professional, to be able to manage these problems in such a way that the function establishes and maintains a reputation for excellent service.

The link with quality

In the last few years, German multinational Robert Bosch has set up its first UK manufacturing subsidiary on a green-field site in South Wales. A policy was adopted from the start of building total quality into all aspects of the operation. According to director of human resources, Martin Wibberley:

> ... total quality clarifies that HR is clearly a management function. No more role ambiguity; no more bridging a gap between management and employees.

At the same time, the function regards the whole organisation as its customer. The approach:[1]

> ... stresses the customer–supplier relationship; every supplier must agree what product or service is to be delivered to the customer, then deliver it 'right first time, on time, and every time'. But this applies not only to the service to our external customers, the car makers, but to our internal customers too. The value of this approach is that it makes everyone aware that we all have customers ... The notion of an internal customer is clearly a demanding notion for HR departments which have not traditionally given enough thought to customer service. It also gives the whole of the organisation the right to specify the service it expects and to comment on delivery, since in HR the whole organisation is our customer. In our organisation, for example, we have developed a customer service index, so that we can repeatedly measure our customers' satisfaction with the service we are delivering.

WORKING THROUGH EMPLOYEES TO DELIGHT THE MARKET-PLACE

At this point, I recall an important injunction of one of the great quality and customer care 'gurus', Dr Edward Deming, who pointed out that focusing on the needs of internal customers is fine, providing it is also in the interests of the 'final' external customer. Internal service must never be to the detriment of the final customer; you should always be able to see clearly how your internal service adds value to the organisation's ultimate product. (Use of the word 'product' reminds me of Deming's dictum about service industries as against manufacturing: 'in the service industry workers do not think they have a product. They just think they have a job. They do have a product – service'.)

This leads me back to the opening theme of this chapter – no less than a claim that the quality of human resource management has a direct impact on customer service, the lifeblood of today's business.

A powerful way of looking at this is described in Richard Schonberger's book *Building a Chain of Customers*. In his preface, the author writes about 'confronting the organisation'. He put it this way:

In large companies, the four main functional groups – design, marketing, accounting/finance, and operations – have scarcely been able to talk to one another. Further, those at the top, middle, and bottom of the organisation have had different concerns and agendas. We need a great cannon that will level the high walls that compartmentalise the business. Donald Petersen, CEO of Ford Motor Company, calls it 'chimney breaking'.

Is there a way to break the chimneys and link the organisation? There is. It's not a cannon, but rather a superordinate goal: serving the customer. Those sound like puff words, unless you hold the enlightened view: that everyone has a customer – at the next process. Linkages from process to process form a chain ending at the next paying customer.

Serving the customer – next in the chain of customers – becomes the overriding goal.

Schonberger is clear about one of the conditions for building a chain of customers – employee involvement. But involvement in what? – 'involvement in everything that is important to the customer – the one at the next process as well as the final one'. A similar notion is expressed by Richard Whiteley in his book *The Customer Driven Company*, where he advocates the need to empower employees to tackle problems that block excellent service. For example, employees must see customer complaints not as something merely to be noted and passed to someone else – the boss, higher authority, the 'complaints department' – but as something that requires proper action now, by them!

He also draws attention to the complementary nature of 'product quality' and 'service quality':

Providing quality as the customer defines it means fully understanding both dimensions of quality: product quality and service quality. If you're a customer, product quality is 'What you get'. Product quality is usually quantifiable. In a manufacturing company, product quality is the reliability and general excellence of the tangible item that goes out the door. In companies that sell services, product quality consists of the tangible, quantifiable aspects of the service: Does your bank statement carry errors? Is the interior of the airplane clean? Is your hotel room well laid-out and does everything in it work? In most organisations product quality is the province of internally focused, analytical, scientific people.

Now, if product quality is the 'What you get' part of the customer's experience, then service quality is the 'How you get it' part. If product quality is tangible, service quality can be described as intangible. Thus, it is often harder to measure than product quality. I can calculate fairly easily how often my product broke down in the first year the customer had it. It's much harder to calculate how clear my instruction manuals were, or how friendly my staff was when customers had problems. But that doesn't make those questions any less important.

British Airways is a case in point. Research conducted by the airline identified staff factors as a major contributor to passenger goodwill. Such factors (attitude, how service was given etc) were quoted by 61 per cent of passengers in the survey as extremely important. On the other hand, only 39 per cent cited other factors, such as timing, food, seating, facilities etc. Even higher at 70 per cent was the number of passengers giving staff factors as the major contributor to any dissatisfaction they may have experienced.

The implications of this were grasped by Midland Bank in their development of a new service strategy in the late 1980s. The bank set up a programme ranging from skills development to workshops on attitudes and values, designed to increase staff appreciation of customer needs and their ability and readiness to respond to them.

But before employees feel ready to be 'empowered' or to accept a role in the front line of service delivery, they must feel valued and well treated. This is not philanthropy, but commercial common sense. There is much evidence to suggest that employees will treat customers in the same way as they themselves feel treated.

The manager's role

Managers are clearly crucial to this issue. The retailer W H Smith conducted research into staff attitudes, and found that for a majority of staff their manager was the single most important factor in determining their attitude towards the firm.

Whiteley links the concept of the role of the manager and the internal client in a striking way. He points out that 'if you are a manager, then every individual in your work group is one of your internal customers. If you are a top manager, then everyone in the company is one of your internal customers.' This leads inexorably to his conclusion 'therefore, treat the people who work for you with the respect you'd give any customers'.

Two sides of the coin for personnel

So the coin of quality and customer service has two sides for personnel. First, lessons about achieving quality apply just as much to personnel as to any other function. So, for example, a personnel service such as payroll has product quality – are the payslips always totally accurate? – and service quality – do the payroll staff respond in a helpful way to staff queries? Secondly, personnel is totally involved in helping the organisation as a whole achieve quality standards.

These are crucial messages for personnel. They bear repeating:

- Personnel must grapple with the absolute need to provide a first class service to their internal clients – dealing convincingly with the conflicting demands that this will involve.
- This internal service must be consciously linked to the ultimate needs of the final customer. It is all about contributing to that chain of customers which will bring sustained success in the market-place.
- Personnel must ensure that the quality of human resource management in the organisation is such that employees share the service vision of the business, strive to delight customers, and are equipped to do so.

Managing for customer service

Schonberger's perspective of an organisation also has important implications for the way the personnel function is managed. For him, real employee involvement means employee ownership of each process. Moreover, this means team ownership:

> Where there is team ownership, team problem-solving and team suggestions should follow. A correctly organised team, which owns a segment in the chain of customers, is called a cell or a flow line: people and their equipment arranged by the way the product flows or the service

is provided. For our customer-serving purposes, team refers to a group of people connected by work flow, because, by definition, that comprises a chain of customers.

Schonberger contrasts this with the traditional approach of grouping people by common function.

> In offices, we may find order-entry people and terminals in the far corner, purchasing in the next room, invoicing downstairs, and so on. In factories, moulding machines are all together in their little world, lathes have their own area elsewhere, and everything else is grouped similarly. Strive for teams and teamwork, and what happens? At best, you get *gangs* – and ganglike behaviors. The customer is part of another gang, and they are the enemy! Or, if not the enemy, they are, at least, not part of your team.

This reminds us of that well-worn expression: 'it would be great here if it weren't for the clients/guests/members – or whatever'. In the case of personnel, 'the staff'! All said jokingly, of course, but many a true word . . .

The personnel gang

Personnel can be just as much a part of this pattern as any other department. The great danger is they form another gang, and indulge in ganglike behaviour. This is understandable, given that personnel is often under fire from all sides, but it won't do. In its attitudes and the way it is organised, personnel must model the chain-of-customer organisation, and help others to follow suit.

Schonberger describes the payoff not only for the company but for individuals:

- staff people who are let out of their offices to team up with front-line employees on mutual concerns are closer to the customer, the source of revenue, the reason for the firm's existence. That's reality.
- In this mode, staff people come to be welcomed by line employees – welcomed for their knowledge and expertise, which is a gratifying change. In the old system, staff advisers were too often resented and sometimes ridiculed for unrealistic 'ivory-tower' advice.
- Experts who learn to work with other experts, and who take career-change assignments, find they are more effective, that the chain of customers is better served. That raises feelings of self-worth.

The marketing alliance

At the start of this chapter, I suggested the possibility of a strategic alliance between personnel and marketing. This involves, as implied in the question above, personnel people walking down the corridor to marketing – or shall we say to those most immediately concerned with developing the firm's relations with customers and the market-place – and teaming up with them.

If delivering superior service to the paying customer is a continuum – from creating the vision to delivery to reviewing performance – personnel has the opportunity to add value at virtually every point on that continuum. Note the word opportunity. Working with the marketing function will not normally appear on your job description, and probably no one will criticise – or even notice – if it doesn't happen. But the opportunity is there to make it happen, and to raise the strategic contribution of the personnel function accordingly.

A checklist

A checklist of action areas might look like this:

- the vision
- selection
- organisation issues
- training
- reward issues
- employee relations
- promoting total quality.

The vision

Is a vision that 'the purpose of business is to make money' calculated to inspire ordinary people to do extraordinary things? Especially to the averagely paid who see large chunks of the money going to others? If personnel has any kind of real business contribution to make, it is surely to do with winning employee commitment. At the heart of such commitment is a vision that is real to everyone in the organisation and to which they are ready to commit themselves. So personnel's task in the vision stakes is twofold – to help the organisation develop a vision that goes beyond profits and financial forecasts, and to ensure it is effectively communicated.

Whiteley lists seven imperatives to produce an organisation that can deliver high quality in both product and service. The first is to 'create a customer-keeping vision' and Whiteley devotes a whole chapter to this imperative. He gives the example of Johnson & Johnson: 'We believe our first responsibility is to doctors, nurses, and patients, to mothers and all others who use our products and services'. This vision was effectively communicated to the company's offices world wide, so that employees at all levels understood that their first obligation was to the customer.

In case any reader is thinking that this is all very well but beyond their level of seniority within their organisation, Whiteley provides action points which could be perfectly relevant to any personnel manager. At the very least, the Personnel function can develop a vision for its own operation that may serve to model what could be achieved for the wider operation.

Selection

To be customer minded implies a certain attitude and ability to maintain a particular set of behaviours. If every employee serves a customer – either internal or external – these attitudes and behaviours assume a new importance in selection profiles. The chief executive of an American bank set out nine beliefs underpinning his management philosophy. The fourth of these was 'hire people who like other people'. This means maintaining a workforce of people who set out enthusiastically to please the customer.

Lawrence Bossidy of Allied Signal made a similar point:[2]

> ... competition is tough, and it takes brains to win. But to-day we look for smart people with an added dimension : they have an interest in other people and derive psychic satisfaction from working with them.

Personnel must surely be in the front line in thinking through the implications for selection if the company is to become truly 'customer driven'.

Organisation issues

Schonberger describes the ultimate form of customer-driven organisation in these terms:

> Small customer/product-focused operator teams, each with its own technical support team, all having a common focus on process control and

improvements; no functional departments; little hierarchy; collapse of line–staff walls.

An increasing number of companies are beginning to reorganise to move in their own way down such a road.

It is clear that the people issues in such developments are legion. Personnel professionals need to establish a thorough knowledge and understanding of the processes involved so that they will be welcome partners in bringing about such fundamental changes in workplace organisation.

Training

A company cannot expect employees to respond effectively to radical new approaches to customer service without training. Here we are on personnel's home territory, but again the function must work alongside line colleagues to identify the best way to help employees deliver the new approach.

Training must recognise the fact that customers want to deal with people who:

- know what they are talking about
- are friendly and able to establish a good rapport
- have enough confidence, common sense and authority to resolve problems personally

Training to develop such staff falls into three categories:

- the 'hard' areas – product knowledge, sales administration and systems
- the 'interpersonal' areas – teamworking, and the classic communicating skills such as listening, questioning and summarising
- the 'empowering' areas – problem-solving, creative thinking and decision-making.

Reward issues

The way people are rewarded passes big messages throughout the organisation. It is taken for granted that knowledge and expertise in the whole area of reward – financial and non-financial – is part and parcel of the personnel professional's toolkit. It is therefore for personnel to ensure that the customer-service-orientation message is clearly reflected in reward policy and practice.

I am not referring here to the reward for salespeople, important though it may be. No, the bigger challenge is how to structure the reward package so that those aspects of the job — of all jobs — that are concerned with service are emphasised and recognised.

We have to search for what Whiteley calls 'customer-driven measurement'. In other words, how do we measure each person's contribution to serving both his or her own customers, and also the company's final customer?

Employee relations – or the way people are treated.

A quote from Tesco: 'there is no point in telling staff to make customers feel special if they themselves don't'. Although the approach of individual managers is of course crucial in this regard, what makes people feel special comes down to the whole range of the company's personnel policies and practice. A number of companies symbolise this by abandoning the word 'employee', which has in their view unfortunate connotations of inferior status and ownership. Terms such as 'associate' are being used to describe staff.

So, both personnel and marketing are keenly interested in ensuring that all the terms of the employment contract in its widest sense — tangible and intangible — are consistent with the concept that all members have a role to play in delivering superior service. This is not a question of 'being nice to your staff' or even listening to them more (although in many organisations this would not be a bad start!). It is a matter of genuinely involving everyone in the customer crusade. This may mean being tough when necessary as not everyone will respond with equal enthusiasm. Some may not be capable of the changes implied.

But here again, the role of personnel is critical, because the way difficulties, and problem staff, are handled will have a major impact on people's commitment.

Promoting total quality

Customer service is inextricably linked with concepts of total quality. The link is clear when we ask the question 'why do we want total quality?', as there is only one valid answer — to provide our customers with the best in both product and service. As we have already noted, quality initiatives often fail just because people within the organisation are not properly integrated into the programme. Schonberger calls it putting the workforce on the attack:

With total quality providing the core agenda, unleash the workforce. Then sit back and watch the fireworks. If you did it right, you will have created an employee-driven improvement engine out of what was formerly seen as a wage-and-benefits sinkhole.

Not only is the personnel function well placed to contribute to such developments, there is no reason why it should not play a central role in getting them off the ground.

CONCLUSIONS

In a study for the European Association for Personnel Management on *The Emerging Role of the HR Manager in Europe*, one survey question probed the views of respondents on the importance of a variety of issues and demands facing business. At the top of the list, with competition and technology, were increasing demands for quality and customer service pressures. The implications were clear. If HR aspired to make a continuing – indeed greater – contribution, it had to develop the capability to be part of the management team confronting those issues.

Being well oriented to serving our own clients is a prerequisite but the real opportunity lies in accepting the challenge of the marketing alliance.

To be strategic, personnel professionals need to have the expertise and sheer courage to empower themselves to make an impact. Nothing of great value was ever achieved by keeping one's head 'below the parapet'.

The implication of this chapter is that 'customer service' must be an essential value of the successful company/organisation. It is also implicit that 'people' values must be regarded as key if personnel is to have a worthwhile role. In fact, the whole issue of values is fundamental to strategic HRM, and we turn to it now in the next chapter.

Key questions

- Who are your prime customers?
- What contribution does the personnel function make to external customer service?
- How can you improve your contribution in these areas?

Notes

1. Wibberley, Martin (1992) 'Why Bosch Went For Total Quality' *Personnel Management* November pp31–2.
2. Tichy, Noel M and Charan, Ram (1995) 'The CEO as Coach – an Interview with Allied Signal's Lawrence A Bossidy *Harvard Business Review* March–April pp70–8.

5

The Importance of Values

" 'The hardest stuff is the soft stuff – values, personal style,
ways of interacting ... if individuals don't change,
nothing changes "
Paul Allair, CE Xerox Corporation

Organisations facing up to change – and seizing the opportunities that
this implies – soon find that the question of values comes high on the
agenda. Values were at the heart of British Airways' well documented
programmes for change, such as 'Winning for customers'. In establishing
a programme for adapting to new market conditions, within which it
needed to launch new products, Glaxo Pharmaceuticals UK focused on
values and beliefs within the company, among other things to reduce
damaging internal competition and to promote flexibility. It identified as
its core values: role clarity, acceptance of change, teamworking, innovation and output orientation. An essential part of the challenge to
reform great institutions such as the National Health Service and the
police force is to imbue people at all levels with a new set of values.

A characteristic of strategic action is that it is 'values driven'. In other
words, it is not simply expedient action to solve an immediate problem,
but is consciously determined to be in line with overriding values that
really matter to the organisation. Moreover, values are the basis of the
behaviour of people in organisations. Personnel professionals need to be
crystal clear on the subject, on what we mean by the word, why the issue
is of importance and what their connection to the issue is.

WHAT DO WE MEAN BY VALUES?

Values represent what is of underlying and fundamental importance to
us. We may or may not be fully aware of them. They may be written

down, but the real test is how they are expressed in action. Someone may say that health is an extremely important core value to them, but continue to smoke heavily – an indicator that in fact other values come higher on that person's list of priorities, whether they recognise it or not. Similarly, within a business the chairman's statement that 'people are our most important asset' may or may not reflect the real core values of that business. Only action tells the true story.

We need to recognise that values exist at two levels: organisational and personal. At the organisational level, they are what leads people to work as a team, or drives them apart; what might be called the glue that holds the organisation together. At a personal level, they will determine the extent to which the individual will give their full loyalty to an organisation. We shall deal with both in this chapter.

In an article on 'How to manage cultural change', consultant Alan Fowler defines values as 'the qualities and characteristics the organisation considers important'.[1] This is as good a working definition as any, but in reality we only come to grips with the subject once we start looking at specific examples, either within our own organisations or elsewhere. Lawrence Bossidy, CEO of Allied Signal:[2]

> ... we spent two days arguing – and I mean arguing – about values. That was helpful because at the end of the meeting, we not only had the values, we also had a specific definition of those values. The seven values we settled on are simple: customers, integrity, people, teamwork, speed, innovation, and performance. They're not unique. But they're important because they give all our people a view of what behavior is expected of them. And if you're a leader in this company, you risk being labeled a hypocrite if you don't behave according to those values. And you're going to get some heat – and I think that's terrific.

WHY DO THEY MATTER TO THE ORGANISATION?

The issue is an essential one for all organisations for three reasons:

- Values are an important determinant as to how a company will operate within a given marketplace; in other words, you must get the values right if the firm is to realise its potential for success.
- Organisations are damaged if disparate and incoherent values are held internally; in other words, management needs to ensure that a common set of these right values are genuinely shared at all levels.
- Values determine whether a business operates in an ethical manner –

and we have seen numerous examples of the damage done to companies by unethical behaviour.

It is also by definition a strategic issue. Values exist or are created for the long term; they are not things which can be switched on and off to suit short term operational requirements. They support the ongoing mission of the business.

In his book *Levers of Control: How Managers Use Innovative Control Systems to Drive Strategic Renewal*, Robert Simons tackled the issue of the tension between control and empowerment. Organisations need flexibility, innovation and creativity, but how to square this with adequate control? Simons suggests four tools to bridge the gap. Three are various mechanisms for measurement, but the fourth is what Simons calls 'beliefs systems'. He recognises that because they are broad, statements of beliefs can often be mere platitudes. But if management adopts them with genuine determination, they can inspire and promote commitment to an organisation's core values and amount to a powerful system of control.

GETTING THE VALUES RIGHT

Values exist in all groups, whether or not they are explicitly recognised. During a period of relative stability, there is little need to identify explicitly what the important values are. They are accepted and by and large unchallenged. It is only when the going gets rough that the need to rethink is recognised. The 1994 HRRC report from Cranfield School of Management, *Different Routes to Excellence* found that the issue of values formed an important part of management thinking in the companies studied.[3] Statements of corporate values took a variety of forms, but were normally in support of some articulation of corporate vision.

In his book on re-engineering, Harvey quotes the case of Bell Atlantic. Following deregulation in the US telecommunications industry, the company had formulated a new strategy. However, the chief executive, Raymond Smith, realised it would get nowhere unless it tackled the obsolete values held by employees. 'There was no unifying concept to rally round. I represented my department, you represented your department and we behaved as if we were opposing lawyers or political opponents.'

Financial services has experienced a radical shake-up in recent years. Among others, the Prudential Corporation has responded in terms of both products and of services, offered and internally. Alongside the company's business strategy, what management has described as a 'corporate context' has been developed, with clear statements of values and beliefs about its three interdependent stakeholders, the customer, shareholder and staff.

One long respected organisation is going through a period of fundamental readjustment. HMSO has recognised that for survival it can no longer rely on its traditional approach. It has to gear up for a more competitive future, and this will involve reorganisation into a number of 'free-standing' businesses. One of a series of communication papers issued to all staff in 1994 tackled the vital issue of values (see Table 5.1).

In a different context, values to be espoused by the IPM (now IPD) were indicated in a statement by the then president, Roger Farrance, as follows:[4]

> The Institute is not the nation's conscience, but its members clearly want it to spell out that people are not just a 'resource' which can be used or discarded in the same way as inanimate plant and capital.

BICC Cables' business in Blackley, Manchester, took the decision to simplify the manufacturing management structure and place more emphasis on teamworking as part of a drive to improve competitiveness. The old supervisory values based on hierarchy were clearly inadequate to sustain such a change and this fact led to the appointment of an entirely new set of team leaders. The selection process took into account the kind of qualities and characteristics which the new way of working would demand, including the following statement under the heading of 'stabilising beliefs':[5]

> *Values:* Enduring beliefs, or assumptions, evidenced by some team leaders and which probably centre around loyalty, conservation, the work ethic and the family. Consistency in value expression strengthens the confidence of colleagues in the team leader because their views are perceived as more predictable and a basis for stability in relationships, even amid organisational change.

SIGNALS FOR CHANGE

What might indicate that current values within the organisation were inadequate or wrong? In some cases, such as HMSO, management will have embarked on a substantial change programme where it has been clear from the start that establishing a new and more relevant set of

Table 5.1 *HMSO communication paper*

The new values we must share

The behaviour expected of a 'good civil servant' in the past is no longer sufficient for success in today's fast moving world. Some things of course remain of continuing importance, perhaps more important than ever. Integrity, objectivity, openness and professionalism are permanent key values.

Directors have concluded that new behaviours also become an essential part of our culture, essential to keep customers and gain and retain jobs in the new free-standing businesses and throughout HMSO.

- *Commitment to delighting customers*; active contribution to the continuous improvement of services and products

- *Being flexible* not rule bound or rigid. Provision of good service comes before 'sticking to procedure'

- *Seeking challenges*; meeting objectives and taking pride in achievement

- *Showing initiative*; not waiting to be told what to do

- *Good team work*; building good relationships with colleagues and offering help and support without being asked

- *Getting it right*; checking your own quality, not relying on others doing it for you

- *Taking responsibility*; for improving service to customers, getting the job done, for one's own job and career, and for the achievements of the team

- *Being eager* to acquire new skills and knowledge

- *Respecting diversity*; seeing customers and colleagues as individuals and being open to new ideas, opinions and approaches

- *Giving confidence* to customers and colleagues

- *Commitment to the business*; taking an interest in the performance and success of the business

- *Doing what we say* we will do when we say we will do it

- *Being professional*; displaying integrity and honesty, looking for opportunities rather than problems, being competent in all aspects of the job

---

Source: Reproduced with the permission of the Controller of HMSO

values was fundamental to the whole exercise. In other cases, the need for change may be indicated in less obvious ways, where in one way or another values currently held internally are out of 'sync' with what the organisation is trying to achieve.

For example, one part of the company may be behaving quite differently from another, and these differences may well signal differing underlying values. In one company, production and sales were working flat out to fulfil a major contract. It became clear that a particular part of the contract would require a special effort from the spare parts department, involving overtime working. This request was turned down, because the manager concerned was imbued with the need to control costs and remain within the overtime budget.

A different example was the case where senior management had spelled out certain core values in a document setting out a new direction for the operation. One aspect was the need for profit centres to work together to create business synergy, leading to new opportunities in the market-place. Unfortunately a number of senior executives continued to behave in the old ways, even to the extent of preferring to see orders going to the competition rather than to internally competing departments. From their particular point of view, this behaviour was perfectly rational because in the past clients had been perceived to have been lost through the failure of those other profit centres. Nevertheless, corporately, new values can never be effectively established unless senior 'role models' are seen to be behaving in tune with them – actions will always speak louder than words.

Another kind of difficulty occurs when the values held by senior management differ markedly from those held by others at more junior levels. This problem was endemic in the old conflictual industrial relations environment, but it would be naive to suppose that it can no longer exist in the brave new world of 'HRM'! Several examples are given elsewhere in this book illustrating that management has to take on board that their employees will have their own agendas which need to be taken into account if the organisation is to achieve cohesion through commonly held values. This kind of issue may become apparent through joint consultation procedures – still alive and well in many companies – or perhaps through regular opinion surveys, or again as a benefit of especially effective two-way communications.

Values and ethical behaviour

We have already mentioned the importance of ethical behaviour in today's climate. Instances where individuals or groups stray into murky waters may be 'one-off' events, or may be a more serious indicator that certain values are only skin deep. British Airways' dispute with Virgin Atlantic over methods used to entice customers has no doubt led to a reappraisal of ethical issues within the company. One personnel director in another organisation was aware that a particular senior executive with responsibility to develop new business was making use of practices that verged on defrauding customers, not to line his own pockets but to increase the profit accruing to the business. During his discussion with the CEO as to what action should be taken, if any, he pointed to the framed Statement of Company Values proudly hanging on the office wall. The response was 'Well, that's all very well but commercial realities must come first'.

HOW TO CHANGE VALUES

Some organisations have chosen a formal route to establishing new values. The steps are:

1. Identify current values, by surveys of employees, customers and suppliers, or by structured interview, by desk research looking at various kinds of internal documentation, or finally simply by senior management's intuitive feel for the company and how it operates.
2. Establish desired future values, perhaps by using similar techniques, or perhaps as part of a strategic planning process.
3. Plan action to achieve change.

Personal example

The action to achieve change varies enormously from one organisation to another. It may be driven in quite a personal way from the top. Former Metropolitan Police Commissioner, Sir Peter Imbert, was instrumental in helping his colleagues to think through the implications of a new kind of police force. This meant seeing the force as a service, and moving away from the old model embracing highly hierarchical and inbred values.

Coherent systems and policies

Where inappropriate values are being driven by particular systems or policies, the obvious route to change is to reform the system or policy in question. If teamworking is seen as a core value, it is essential that the reward system reflects this. If it does not, change is unlikely to happen without a change in reward policy. A new reward system clearly implying teamworking as an essential skill for all managers is likely to have a significant impact.

An engineering company, Barr and Stroud, had operated for many years on traditional lines, but recognised the need to change.[6] Management worked successfully to revolutionise industrial relations procedures and to forge a new relationship with the workforce. This was symbolised by new practices in communications and terms and conditions of employment. In other words, the company did not just tamper with one aspect of policy, but recognised the need to change the whole system. The new approach was coherent and gave consistent messages to the workforce. It successfully communicated a new way of working, based on a new set of values.

Author Richard Whiteley[7] compiled a list of what it might mean to become a 'customer-driven' organisation. (see Table 5.2). Many of the changes imply new values.

The developmental route

For some companies, the most appropriate route will be a developmental one. Workshops will be held with groups of managers and others to thrash out the operational implications of the new values. In one financial services company, a department responsible for producing documentation such as invoices and cash flow reports invited to their workshops representatives from their client departments. These representatives were asked to come to the event armed with responses from their own colleagues to four questions:

1. Do you agree with our statement of objectives?
2. In what ways do we provide a good service?
3. In what ways could our service be improved?
4. How could you help us to provide a better service?

All the representatives responded that the hardest question to answer was question 2 – none of their colleagues could say in what ways the

Table 5.2   *Becoming a customer-driven organisation*

From	To
Motivation through fear and loyalty	Motivation through shared vision
An attitude that says, 'it's their problem'	Ownership of every problem that affects the customer
'The way we've always done it'	Continuous improvement
Making decisions based on assumptions and judgment calls	Doing it with data and fact-finding decisions
Everything begins and ends with management	Everything begins and ends with customers
Functional 'stovepipes' where departments base decisions solely on their own criteria	Cross-functional cooperation
Being good at crisis management and recovery	Doing it right the first time
Depending on heroics	Driving variability out of the process
A choice between participative or scientific management	Participative *and* scientific management

Source: Whitely 1991, reproduced by kind permission of the publishers

department concerned provided a good service! Needless to say, they were full of ideas as to how the service could be improved. While the issues on the surface were operational ones, the real problem was one of values, about the way backroom operations were perceived, virtually regardless of performance. The workshop succeeded in bringing the values issue on to the corporate agenda, and the firm was able to move on from there.

Assessing individuals

Sometimes managers are so imbued with the old ways that they are unable to change. Even where they might be able to do so, it may be felt that fresh faces are needed to force people to take the changes seriously. In these situations the main approach to establishing different values is by means of new people in key roles. At Barr and Stroud, around 22 out of 40 executives left or were fired over a period of five years. The most important feature of the change programme at BICC Cables' Blackley site was the development of a new role of team leader, dispensing with the old roles of supervisor and charge hand. Existing supervisors and charge hands were invited to apply but appointment as one of the new team leaders was not guaranteed.

The informal approach

Life is often less clear cut than is assumed in textbooks! The realisation of the importance of values, or of the need to change them, often emerges as change proceeds. Indeed, if we hold the view that now nothing is constant except change the idea of a change programme creating a period of stability is a contradiction in terms. So while values do by definition endure, they may well undergo continuing review and refinement.

This may emerge from other processes, as an important by-product, perhaps without management being fully cognisant of it in advance. Alternatively, management may feel cautious as to what values would emerge as key to their future developments. In reviewing the dramatic changes put through over a period of time by the Prudential Corporation, director of personnel Geoff Keyes recognised quite frankly that 'values involving staff were not articulated at the beginning of the process – as perhaps in theory they should – but rather as a post-event rationalisation.'[8]

HOW PERSONNEL CAN CONTRIBUTE

So far in this chapter, we have highlighted some of the issues surrounding the question of values. We need now to be specific about the role that personnel may play.

'Guardian of core values'

There is a strong case that personnel is the function best placed to act in this guardian capacity. It involves:

- having a clear idea as to what the core values are and what they mean
- monitoring policies and management practice to ensure they support these values

- surveying the organisation, in an informal or formal way, to check out employee understanding
- keeping in close touch with line management, to be an advocate of the value system
- using the values as a touchstone when tackling specific problems.

In many organisations, the core values may be implied rather than written down. This need not be a problem, particularly if the values strongly imbue the organisation. Personnel may be well aware of what the values are and share this understanding with colleagues and staff generally.

On the other hand, if the value system is less well inculcated within the organisation, personnel may have a more delicate task. The function may have its own ideas as to what are the 'right' values for the organisation, and is in a good position to advocate and reinforce them. In fact, personnel will often find itself in a 'missionary' role. Danger can arise if such a role gets too far out of step with attitudes and values elsewhere within the management team.

Personnel may be called on to challenge the actions and decisions of line management if these are clearly in opposition to core values. This requires considerable political skill. The question will arise as to how far the issue is negotiable and to what extent it is appropriate to compromise in the light of commercial reality.

It is of course when the going gets tough that an effective statement of values is important. Where the values are well regarded and understood, the statement is simply in place for occasional reference and to act as a reminder. It is when a really difficult issue arises that the statement comes into its own. It is then that the organisation finds out whether the values are a reality.

One area where personnel's contribution is indisputable is the way the personnel department itself is managed. Personnel has no hope of building and reinforcing values within the wider company if they are not practised 'in house'. But when this is done, the function is an important role model for the organisation as a whole.

From 'guardian' to 'conscience'

There is an extension to the guardian role. Company values are of two types. The first is where no external moral or ethical yardsticks are involved. One company stated as one of its core values 'creating a flexible, adaptable organisation, free from artificial demarcation, where people are free to innovate and experiment'. While this was no doubt of great importance to that firm, such a value has no intrinsic moral or ethical basis.

On the other hand, another of the values stated quite categorically: 'We conduct our affairs with uncompromising honesty and integrity. We aim to be an intellectual and social asset for the local community in every country in which we trade.' Although such a core value was included to support the company's commercial interest – a phrase such as 'licence to operate' comes to mind – the value itself is of a different order from the first one. Action out of step with creating a flexible organisation is not morally reprehensible in itself, whereas dishonest conduct is liable to censure, especially if it gets into the public domain.

Here personnel is moving from the guardian of established company values to the 'conscience' of the company. This is a more hazardous role, especially when short term commercial interest is involved. It is in areas like this that one faces the fact that personnel is far from being the soft option which is sometimes portrayed. Where real ethical or moral issues are at stake, personnel is on the line.

During the course of one training workshop in a fast moving financial institution, a leading business producer announced that he 'would be prepared to slit my grandmother's throat for another grand of sales'. While the comment was (presumably) meant in jest, it indicated a mindset that could cause the firm substantial difficulty. The trainer used the occasion to challenge the thinking behind the comment and draw out its contrast with the stated values of the firm.

The importance of this has been amply illustrated in recent times. A widely reported example is the situation in the life and pensions field, with many sales forces in life companies attracting criticism from the regulator and the public for their selling methods.

Personnel as advocate

Personnel is well placed to recognise and advocate the need for a restatement of values. Circumstances where this may be needed include:

- where the core values are confused and ill defined
- where they have been well established but are now inadequate for an evolving business strategy

- where they are enunciated but not carried through in practice
- where there are conflicting values in different parts of the organisation.

From values to action

Companies may be faced with situations where values are clear and accepted but where the action needed to implement them is less clear. In his second *Trouble Shooter* book, Sir John Harvey-Jones identifies just such a situation in the South Yorkshire Police. Statement of Purpose and Values (see Table 5.3). The author has no argument with the sentiments expressed. As he says: 'They outline very clearly the sort of police force I would wish to pay for and the ways in which I would expect such a force to behave.' On the other hand:

> ... when I imagined myself as a policeman reading the documents, I found myself wondering what the document told me about where my priorities lay and how the apportionment of money and effort would be made. The documents are a description of how things should be done rather a clear definition of what needs to be done.

Table 5.3 *The South Yorkshire Police Statement of Purpose and Values*

Our purpose on behalf of the general public is:

- to uphold the Rule of Law
- to keep the Queen's Peace
- to prevent and detect crime
- to protect life and reassure people in need.

Our values. In achieving our purpose, we must at all times strive to:

- act fairly within the law, serving with integrity the ends of justice
- act fairly and reasonably, without fear or favour and without prejudice of any kind
- ensure that the rights of all citizens – especially the vulnerable – are safeguarded, regardless of status, race, colour, religion, sex or social background
- be courageous in facing physical danger or moral challenge
- be honest, courteous and tactful in all that we do and say
- use persuasion, common sense and good humour wherever possible as an alternative to the exercise of force and, if force is finally necessary, to use only that which is necessary to accomplish our lawful duty.

Source: Harvey-Jones 1992

One may object that that is precisely what values are all about – how things should be done. Nevertheless, personnel may play a useful role in helping people to be clear about the implications of values for action.

Using the right people

Unhappily, some people may never be able to respond to the new situation, particularly where long cherished values have to change. Personnel will need to ensure that such employees are helped to leave the organisation in a dignified way. More constructively, personnel has the responsibility to ensure that the right criteria are being used for selection of new staff, and are being applied competently.

One supermarket chain opened a major new site and was determined to employ staff with the potential to deal with customers and to act on their own initiative. Given the fact that it was a green-field site, an enormous number of applicants applied and it would have been easy to fill the vacancies many times over. In fact the company interviewed 2500 people to fill 150 jobs. Personnel took a lead in creating a highly successful operation.

In 1993, Rhone Poulenc decided that its whole pharmaceutical sales operation had to be re-engineered to respond to new conditions in the health care market.[9] The sales force had to learn to negotiate at a senior level in hospitals and for this far more entrepreneurial freedom was necessary than had been traditional in the past. The traditional regional sales manager position was redefined as that of a regional business manager, involving not only new skills but also a completely new approach to the job. Existing staff had to be assessed and given the opportunity to take on board the values inherent in these radical changes.

The choice and management of consultants

In the Rhone Poulenc case, external consultants were employed to advise on the change process. The relationship between management and consultants can often go horribly wrong, with the company paying out large sums of money for little obvious return. Personnel can add real value by helping to ensure that the right consultants are chosen, with clear and measurable terms of reference, and that the programme is constantly monitored and kept on track.

The personal skills required to make these various contributions are of a high order. One situation will demand skills of analysis, definition and reflection. Another will be more action oriented – actually getting things done.

METHODS

The power of questions ...

One way of getting people to think about values is to ask pertinent questions. Examples might be:

- What does our value statement tell us about the kind of appraisal scheme we should have?
- What does it tell us about the role of managers in our organisation?
- What are its implications for the way we treat mistakes made by staff?

Such questions push people to think through the implications for themselves.

... and when you can ask them

Personnel has plenty of opportunity to put such questions. It may be at the executive committee, or during informal coaching sessions with individual managers. It could be as part of presentations of documentation to communicate the value statement, or during training events.

In the case of one high street bank, the personnel manager became aware during training sessions of a growing unease among staff, generated by the pace of change, and a sense that no one understood the rationale for the changes. Attempts to alert top management of the need for more effective communication processes fell on stony ground. The response tended to be of the 'well you would say that wouldn't you' variety.

Finally, the chief executive agreed to attend a social event at the end of a training workshop. In response to a well planted question, one of the participants had the courage to blurt out that staff were losing trust in the bank. For a bank, trust is a value at the very heart of its whole raison d'être, and the comment so stung the top man that he immediately instituted a series of communication meetings to be chaired by him.

Skilled personnel practitioners know there is more than one way of making strategic progress – even if it sometimes means that the credit has to go elsewhere.

The use of attitude surveys ...

Attitude surveys are another tool appropriate for personnel to use in promoting understanding and debate about the values of the company. Carefully worded items on the survey can test the links between values, policy implications and management practice.

... And training

Apart from providing the chance to raise questions, there is often a place for training events specifically designed to communicate values, especially where management is trying to introduce new values and to make some kind of break with the past. Simply to inform employees about this is likely to be ineffective. Personnel practitioners should be able to deploy their skills to bring people into the process of thinking through the reality and implications of the new values; people need to grasp what the changes might mean for them personally.

EMPLOYEES AND VALUES

There have been two themes in this chapter so far:

1. The establishment of appropriate values is a critical strategic issue for organisations, particularly at times of extensive change.
2. The personnel function can, and should, make a big contribution in this field.

There is a third theme we need to identify. How does the issue of values look from the employee's perspective?

In this section, I propose to follow two strands of thought. First, for employees to give of their best, they need to find some meaning in their work; they need to be able to make sense of the firm and their part in it. Secondly, employees have their own values, which they do not leave behind at the factory gate, or office entrance. How do these square up with the values of their employer?

People need meaning in their work

In a case study of Ford Motor Company, by Ken Starkey and Alan McKinlay, the authors reiterate the view that human resource management is the key factor in understanding Japanese success.[10] They recall Deming's emphasis on purpose at work and worker self-respect as sources of competitiveness. The conventional Western approach creates obstacles so that 'the hourly worker is deprived of his right to do good work and to be proud of himself'. This, according to Deming, 'may be the single most important contribution of management to poor quality and loss of market'. The alternative to the conventional Western approach based on scientific management is to create opportunities for the pursuit of meaning in work. Work arrangements should, therefore, emphasise trust, teamwork and the opportunities to develop creative, problem-solving and co-operative capabilities.

The case describes Ford as on the brink of disaster in the late 1970s. A new mission statement embodying company strategy was enunciated in 1984. Basic values were 'people, products and profits'. All strategic issues – quality, customer satisfaction and cost reduction – depended 'on the capacities, competencies and commitment of our people'. Previous philosophy held that problems of quality control derived from the failure of workers to conform to management directives; the new approach turned this way of thinking on its head. The problems had actually stemmed from management practices. The authors conclude that: ... the troubles were seen as firmly rooted not just in problems of the business cycle and in the new competition but in lack of trust between management and labour, a lack of clear corporate values and sharply defined goals.

The importance of sharing values

Another case is the example of Tioxide UK which implemented far-reaching changes during the 1980s. At first sight, these could be regarded as an inevitable response to external factors, such as changing markets and new techologies. But problems of quality and failing technology, with low levels of employee involvement and skill had been a feature of the company since the 1970s. What drove the changes in the 1980s were the values, judgments and perceptions of key decision-makers, who saw their organisational world in a quite different light from their predecessors.

Fundamental to the mindset of these new managers was the absolute imperative to create shared values and common loyalties throughout the organisation. Translated into action this meant teamworking, participation, cooperation, and skills development. Significantly, change began with the reform of managerial work, symbolising the close of the 'them and us' era.

Earlier in this chapter we discussed the definition and implementation of appropriate values by management and how personnel can add value to the process. What we learn from the Ford and Tioxide cases is how vital it is for management to view the world as seen by employees. Without this insight, genuinely shared values will never be achieved.

What about the individual's values?

This leads us to the final strand in this chapter – the relationship between organisational and individual values. In his *Handbook of Personnel Management Practice*, Armstrong provides a sample 'Statement of Core Values'. Two of these are:

- *Partnership* – all employees are treated as partners in the enterprise, to be involved in matters that affect them and to be told the results and future plans.
- *People* – employees are treated fairly and as responsible human beings. They are given the opportunity to develop their skills and careers, and the firm is constantly aware of the need to improve the quality of their working lives.

A clear implication of such a statement is that the values of each individual employee will be respected, presumably even where they differ from those of the organisation. True partners must have some space to nurture the things that are dear to them not just in their private lives but within the workplace.

Back to balance

Indeed, in his 'headings for values checklist', Armstrong's very first item is 'balance between needs of organisation and staff'. In fact there is nothing new about this. The concept is an integral part of some of the early definitions of personnel management. Yet the reality in many organisations today is very different. An example which comes immediately to mind is the way some firms approached the controversial matter of Sunday trading.

The more hard-nosed manifestations of HRM imply that everyone must be imbued with *management* values – there is no room for debate and the concept of balance is anathema. In these circumstances, it is hard to see how there can be 'partnership' in any real sense.

Individuals in a competitive world

How can an organisation make room for a whole variety of individual values in a competitive world? This was one of the issues confronted by consultants Buck Blessing and Tod White, who designed their work round certain basic beliefs. Some of these are:

- Individuals have the primary responsibility for their own development and job satisfaction.
- Productivity improvement increasingly depends on the performance of individuals.
- The energy for performance improvement is generated by commitment to personal motivators.

One of the distinctive features of the prime Blessing White programme, 'Managing Personal Growth', is that it focuses strongly on personal values and how they relate to the job. Too often companies ignore employees' own values, in their eagerness to communicate those of the employer. Yet Blessing and White are surely correct that people are motivated by their own way of seeing the world and what is important to them.

A Blessing White consultant, Stephen Parker, sees it like this:[11]

> There has been a collapse of loyalty to the organisation. Many that espoused 'employment for life' have had layoffs and downsizing. The ensuing insecurity forces individuals to look out for themselves. If senior management is insensitive to the human cost of these turbulent times, then it will breed further cynicism and withholding of discretionary effort. That is, the energy, time and creativity which can only be volunteered by individuals, not commanded by the organisation, which is the life blood of a successful company.

Noel Tichy of the University of Michigan School of Business summarised what is involved if employers are to take seriously the need for genuinely shared values:[12]

I'm convinced that the most effective competitors in the twenty-first century will be organisations that learn how to use shared values to harness the emotional energy of employees. It calls for emotional commitment. You can't get it pointing a gun. You can't buy it, no matter how much you pay. You've got to earn it, by standing for values that other people want to believe in, and by consistently acting on those values, day in and day out.

CONCLUSION

I started this chapter by stating that personnel professionals need to have a thorough grasp of the issues surrounding the question of values within organisations. Values are a crucial strategic area, central to effective human resource management. Those who aspire to make strategic impact need to be in there, evaluating what is needed, influencing decision-makers, and helping the organisation to live out the right values through consistent policy and practice.

The issue of values may not necessarily be in the personnel manager's job description, but this does not mean that the opportunity is not there. Personnel has the chance to move on to the high strategic ground on values in an entrepreneurial way. But to do it requires skill and sensitivity, and in many situations considerable courage.

Key questions

- Does your organisation have a statement of core values?

- Is there congruence between the organisation's stated values and policy and practice?

- What role does the personnel function have in defining, promoting or maintaining the values of the organisation?

Notes

1. Fowler, Alan (1993) *PM Plus*, Nov p25.
2. Tichy, Noel M and Charan, Ram (1995) 'The CEO as Coach – an Interview with Allied Signal's Lawrence A Bossidy' *Harvard Business Review* March–April pp70–8.
3. Tyson, S and Doherty, N (1994) *Different Routes to Excellence* HRRC report Cranfield School of Management.

4. Farrance, Roger (1993) 'Establishing Standards of Professional Competence' *Personnel Management* October p6.

5. Bott, Keith and Hill, Dr Jonathan (1994) 'Change Agents Lead the Way' *Personnel Management* August pp24–7.

6. Pickard, Jane (1993) 'From Strife to Smooth Sailing' *Personnel Management* December pp38–41.

7. Whiteley, Richard (1991) *The Customer Driven Company* Addison-Wesley.

8. Keyes, Geoff (1993) 'A Prudent Approach to Corporate Renewal' *Personnel Management* October pp54–7.

9. An Oxford Training case study.

10. Starkey, Ken and McKinlay, Alan *Strategy and Human Resource*, see Bibliography.

11. With acknowledgement to consultants Blessing White of St Mark's Road, Windsor.

12. Tichy, Noel and Devanna, Mary Anne *The Transformational Leader*, see Bibliography.

Part Three

Getting Down to Action

We need to take a realistic view of what is possible. The best plans of action are those which enable us to get going. They are not usually a total blueprint to enable us to move from A to B in one fell swoop, but they do ensure that we make a start.

The biggest danger is inertia and putting off what we can do today to a 'better' time. All our experience tells us that there will never be a better time; if we are too busy or under too much pressure to start being more proactive today, we know in our heart of hearts that things will be no easier tomorrow or the next day. Those who seriously wish to develop their influence and their career in a strategic way had better start now! This part of the book sets out some practical ways to do this.

With process comes task. What are likely to be your priorities? Because personnel people are so busy, they need to be quite clear about priorities. Priorities within organisations are changing and personnel activity must respond to this new agenda. What are the tasks that are most important for the future of organisations? How is best practice shaping up in these areas? If in the spirit of total quality and continuous improvement only the best will do, what does it take to establish policies and practices that are world class?

Leadership is vital in any sphere and personnel is no exception. What is the role of the HR director in today's organisations and what are the skills and attributes needed to fulfil it successfully? Is the HR director likely to be appointed from the professional ranks of the personnel function or are these appointments increasingly from the line? How can you prepare yourself to exercise leadership at the top level?

6

Process – How to Develop a Strategic Approach

"Control your destiny – or someone else will".
Jack Welch, General Electric

The main purpose of this book is to help practising personnel managers to develop a strategic approach to their work, to their organisation and to their career. So far we have set the strategic scene and have identified some of the critical issues to be tackled. We turn now to the process of developing a personnel strategy.

It must be emphasised that we are not attempting here to propose a fully fledged planning process to be applied to a business overall. What this chapter sets out is a model designed to enable you to start moving down the strategic road in a practical way. The question posed at the opening of the book was 'Where do you want to be in two years' time?' It was suggested that many personnel managers respond that they would wish to be 'more part of the management team' or 'more involved in the management decision-making process'.

POTENTIAL OBSTACLES

There are various difficulties for personnel managers developing a strategic approach. These include:

● *Workload* There are so many problems and demands being thrown on a daily basis at the average personnel department, that it becomes difficult to see the wood for the trees. Those concerned are forced into a reactive and often administrative mode. There seems to be no realistic opportunity to sit back, and to take stock.

- *Resources* This may be linked to a lack of resource, particularly in a climate of cost cutting, where personnel may be regarded as an overhead, as compared to revenue producing departments.
- *Line support* There may well be little understanding among line management as to the potential contribution of the personnel function, and hence little support for strategic initiatives.
- *Organisation strategy* Those organisations which establish a genuine strategic view of the future are in the minority. It will not be easy for the personnel manager to think through his or her own strategic vision if such thinking is absent in terms of the business overall.
- *Professional experience* The personnel manager concerned may be unsure of how to go about strategic development, and would prefer to remain within the traditional comfort zone of systems and operational problem-solving.

Make a start

Nevertheless, even where some or all of these obstacles exist, there is always scope to start moving down the strategic road. It may take time, and may never achieve the level of sophistication that might be desirable in an ideal world, but the rewards will be considerable, in terms of personal satisfaction and of real contribution. What is indispensable is the will and determination to make a start, and perhaps to take risk.

THE MODEL PHASE 1: ENSURING SERVICE EXCELLENCE

The model presented in Figure 6.1 is intended to be thoroughly practical and to be flexible enough to suit most situations.

As already discussed, personnel needs to delight its customers. This is no easy task, particularly as experience shows that the department is an easy scapegoat when things go wrong. Many personnel people have to contend with the fact that in less good times managers are laying the problems at their door: 'we don't recruit the right people' or 'if only we could train our people properly' or 'our employment costs are too high/ we are not paying enough to keep the right people'. In good times, it is of course a different story; line managers are fully aware of the success of the latest sales drive, or the increase in market share owing to that great new product, but somewhat less inclined to recognise personnel's contribution.

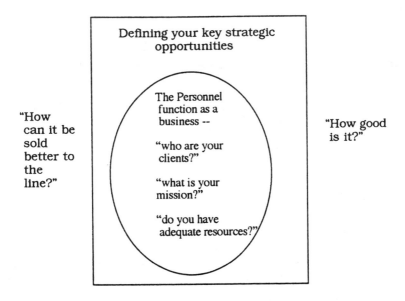

Figure 6.1 *A model for developing strategic excellence in personnel*

Enough of this scepticism! Still, you are clearly not in the best position to advocate a sophisticated new approach to succession planning if the MD is dissatisfied with his or her new secretary. So service excellence is the indispensable platform on which to build the strategic function.

Measuring core services

The model suggests that you take the core services being provided by personnel, and subject them one by one to analysis.

Here we run immediately into one of the perennial problems of the personnel function. There are two schools of thought. The first follows the dictum that 'if it can't be measured, it can't be managed – therefore measure everything in sight'. The second is at the other extreme, setting out the proposition that searching for personnel measures is on the whole a fruitless exercise, and time would be better spent improving the business.

We need to distinguish two categories of measurement. The first might be described as technical measures, and the second as business measures. The former are primarily at the level of personnel proficiency. For instance, 'our plan predicated recruitment of 30 graduates on time and to budget'. Or again, the number of trainees processed through a particular course during the year. These clearly beg questions as to the quality of the graduates recruited, and the effectiveness of the training against business needs. Another example might be:

1. All appraisal interviews to be completed within three months, with the required returns to personnel [a 'technical' measure].
2. All action identified under the heading of training needs to be completed within the year [a 'technical' measure].
3. Structured interviews to be held with a sample of managers and staff three months after the appraisal to ascertain their reactions [dependent on the questions asked, more business oriented, but subjective].

Even measures such as labour turnover and absenteeism are often of limited value and interest to business managers. Labour turnover may simply be a function of current labour market conditions – no surprise if turnover dropped dramatically in the early '90s – and absenteeism may also be subject to various influences more or less outside management's control.

Another problem with routine personnel measures is that many line managers take little interest in them. Considerable time and effort may be put into providing professional personnel returns, which are then churned out as part of monthly figures and regarded by most recipients as fodder for the waste bin. Whether this is a good use of valuable personnel resource is arguable.

This is not to say however that measurement is a waste of time – far from it. But the effort must be carefully targeted. The most effective measures will be those most oriented to business needs, expressed in business terms and hence of most interest to recipients. And it is these that are more likely to be truly strategic. Here are a few tips.

The how and why idea

Take any personnel process and ask two questions: how we propose to do this, and why we are doing it? The answer to the first question is written above the description of the activity, and the answer to the why question is written below it. Now address the 'how' question to the top answer, and the 'why' question to the bottom one, and continue the process. Sooner or later, the top answer will read, just get on with it, while the bottom one will read, to improve profitability. The model is then completed.

It provides insights as to how the issue might be tackled. But it also indicates the point in this hierarchy where measurement might be most telling. Figure 6.2 gives a highly simplified illustration.

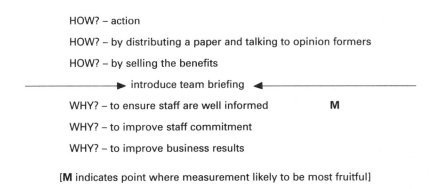

HOW? – action

HOW? – by distributing a paper and talking to opinion formers

HOW? – by selling the benefits

——————————▶ introduce team briefing ◀——————————

WHY? – to ensure staff are well informed   **M**

WHY? – to improve staff commitment

WHY? – to improve business results

[**M** indicates point where measurement likely to be most fruitful]

Figure 6.2   *Analysing a process*

Identify core elements

It may not be necessary to measure every aspect of the function concerned. As in benchmarking, the most cost effective approach is to identify core elements and concentrate effort on them.

In the case of one personnel department in a financial services firm there was evidence of dissatisfaction with regard to the recruitment service being offered. Personnel surveyed their line management customers and identified the one element in the process which was at the heart of the problem. There was no dissatisfaction as far as the end result was concerned – staff were being recruited to the desired quality at an appropriate cost – but there was intense frustration during the process because line managers were not kept informed on progress. There was what personnel called a 'black hole' during the recruitment process, when the customer felt in the dark as to what action was being taken. In some situations this might not be viewed as especially serious but in these circumstances the survey revealed that the black hole was damaging personnel's credibility.

Action was taken to tackle the issue and over a period of time customers were specifically asked about this aspect at the conclusion of every recruitment exercise. The standard negotiated with line management colleagues was that no manager should complain about this feature over a six month period, and the issue was included in a report at the end of that period to all those who had been surveyed.

Ad hoc and one off

One training manager has used the 'Investors in People' process to establish the principle of measurement throughout the organisation. When personnel or training has made a specific contribution, he does not hesitate to ask his line colleagues to put a value on it in financial terms – in writing. One presentation about the people capabilities of the firm helped to win an important order, and the marketing manager put a value on this of £125,000.

I believe Personnel regularly adds substantial value, but we are all too busy doing the next job to take time out to get a valuation and record it. If personnel is doing the right things well and in a cost effective way, the total recorded by the end of the year would indicate a highly satisfactory rate of return; probably higher than many of the organisation's other investments.

Use business ratios

Personnel departments need to use the language of business. This means finding appropriate quantifiable measures. A whole range of measures are available (for example in a book such as *Evaluating the Personnel Function* by Tyson and Fell). The trick is to identify key ones which line managers can immediately identify as relevant to the business.

But don't be afraid of subjective measures

It is best to face the fact that quantifiable measures are not available for all aspects of the work of personnel. This does not mean that no measurement is available. In many instances, what matters is how people feel about things – in other words they make intuitive judgements.

Far more could be said on the topic of measurement, but hopefully enough is given in this section to indicate ways forward.

How good is it? – assessing activities

It is one thing to measure an activity, another to assess how good it is. For example, in Henley's 1992 Business Survey of the 'Golden Triangle', 63 per cent of respondents spent between 1 per cent and 2 per cent of turnover on training. A measured result, but disappointing compared to a reported European *average* of 2 per cent, let alone to the level of investment of world class businesses, which spend many times that amount. Perhaps the question should be 'is it good enough?' which implies testing the measured result against some desired objective or benchmark. The various approaches to tackling this question are summarised below.

Internal audit of customer satisfaction

There are a number of tools in the market for conducting a formal audit. For example, the analytical survey adopted by the Personnel Standards Lead Body indicates the views of both personnel and line on each aspect of personnel activity comparing the degree of importance with the level of satisfaction. This brings focus on to those areas which are important and less than fully satisfactory.

Alternatively, an approach pioneered by consultants MCP compares the level of importance given by internal customers to a given activity with the cost and time devoted to it.[1] As illustrated in Figure 6.3, the position in each quartile is:

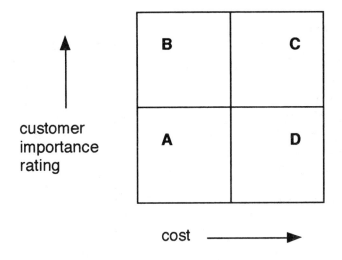

Figure 6.3 *The cost/value matrix*

A.   Low importance, low cost – no further consideration required
B.   High importance, low cost – it ain't broke, so don't fix it!
C.   High importance, high cost – looks like money well spent, but reducing cost could be a bonus
D.   Low importance, high cost – ouch!

Benchmarking

This has the advantage of comparing your current practice with practice in other organisations. It can range from informal exchanges between professional colleagues from different companies, to a formal survey (again, MCP have a firmly established tool available in the market).

Use of qualitative measures

A whole range of measures may be adopted. What is important is that this is done as part of a conscious policy and sustained over a period of time. The approach is not dissimilar to ways in which any organisation might monitor quality.

Attitude/opinion surveys

Personnel is normally in a good position to influence the content of such surveys. This can provide the opportunity to test the quality of various personnel activities.

One personnel manager issued a questionnaire to all staff after their first month in the job as part of the induction process. This was sustained every month for a period of three years. Quite apart from its value in induction, it proved to be a useful way of monitoring the effectiveness of personnel activity. For example, one question related to the attitudes of supervisors, as perceived by the new recruits. At the beginning of the period, it was clear that supervisors were highly task oriented – staff would hesitate to discuss problems with them other than those strictly related to the task in hand. A parallel initiative was supervisory training, and over a period of time the response to the induction questionnaire changed markedly. Some years later, a company attitude survey indicated that relationships between staff and supervisors were excellent.

Professional judgment

One problem with asking internal customers about the service they receive, is that the managers concerned may have a somewhat primitive idea of what to expect from a personnel function. Alternatively, personnel may be engaged in policies which are less than universally popular because they restrict the freedom of managers to act unilaterally. Sometimes therefore, the personnel manager has to fall back on his or her professional judgment. This may be a part of doing the right thing and sticking to one's guns. Nevertheless, some other corroboration is important from time to time – hence the need to ask at regular intervals 'how well are we doing?' and 'is it good enough?'

How can we improve?

A vital aspect of adopting a strategic approach is for the function to embrace a philosophy of continuing improvement. Any personnel department which is resting on its laurels is already in decline!

The difficulty here is not so much with the theory but with the application: how to embark on the road to real improvement when work pressures are already intense and resources are cut to the bone? There are no easy answers, although experience indicates that achieving continuing improvement is above all an attitude of mind.

In one case, there was a history of constant recourse to disciplinary procedures. This was considered part of the natural order of things, despite being extremely time consuming, with a negative impact on relationships. More than a dozen cases at a time were not uncommon and it was apparent that managers saw the procedure as the way to get rid of difficult employees. Personnel determined not to accept that nothing could be done, and instituted a sustained practice of coaching managers to deal more constructively with each individual case. Over a number of years, the number of such cases dwindled until a formal case became a rarity. At the same time it was no coincidence that the personnel department was quite regularly asked to undertake staff counselling.

In another organisation, personnel was burdened with a flow of individual queries requiring resolution. Each case was decided on its merits; a reasonable approach in its way, but extremely time consuming. The personnel director decided that the position called for a series of written policies agreed by management. Once these had been established, many of the individual cases were decided by the line without recourse to personnel. To achieve this improvement required intense effort by personnel not only in terms of preparing proposed policies but arguing them through to gain the acceptance of senior line colleagues.

Both cases indicated a determination on the part of personnel not to accept the status quo, but to win improved ways of operating. Although both initiatives demanded considerable investment of precious personnel time in the early stages the investment proved to be sound. It ultimately led to better ways of working for the organisation, and equally to a more productive use of personnel resource.

How can it be sold better to the line?

We have already discussed in an earlier chapter the question of personnel and its customers, but the essential point bears repeating. A major trap for personnel is that because we know we are doing a good job for the organisation we assume that our efforts are well appreciated by line colleagues and by management. What's more, we are so busy beavering away that we do not make time to check this assumption out. Sadly, we are often labouring under a serious misapprehension – something which some people only find out once it is too late to retrieve matters.

In fact, the opposite assumption must be made, namely that line managers do not hold personnel in high regard unless they take positive and continuing action to sell themselves. This in turn assumes that they have a good story to sell, and that will depend on how successfully they *ensure service excellence*.

To reiterate the process

For *each* key process for which we are responsible:

- How is it measured?
- How good is it? Is it good enough?
- How can it be improved?
- How can it be sold better to the line?

THE MODEL PHASE 2: DEFINING STRATEGIC OPPORTUNITIES

Providing excellent personnel service is a prerequisite for achieving a more strategic approach. It provides a good platform – *but it is not in itself sufficient*. The platform must be used to build a truly strategic approach.

First – some kind of vision

Building personnel strategy is similar to general business strategic thinking, as debated in the opening chapter. It requires some kind of vision of where you want to take the function, yet needs flexibility in implementation. It is like aiming for a mountain peak – you will certainly come across unforeseen obstacles on the way (like for example a bog!) and will have to modify your plan accordingly, but the desired peak remains in view.

Intuitive as well as rational ...

Establishing a vision is not entirely a rational process; it also requires an intuitive feel and a sense of where your opportunities lie. It has something in common with a sense of placement in sport. One tennis champion spoke about this in these terms:

> I learned placement years ago in tennis. You have sort of a mental picture where you want the ball to go or land before you hit it with your racquet or hand. I use the same principle with my short shots and putting in golf. In other words, when I face the green and before I swing my club, I have an instant mental picture of where I want the ball to land.

He also adds 'of course, a proper stance, knowledge of handling the clubs, and so forth, are vital'.

... and entrepreneurial

Developing strategy is also in its own way an entrepreneurial process, and implies a desire to break out from the status quo.

In her book *Choices for the Manager*, Rosemary Stewart discusses whether managers are 'steered or carried along'. Although 'a manager is traditionally described as someone who does the planning, as well as organising and motivating', she states that 'most of the managers whom we studied say that they are not normally conscious of choice'. Clearly, if a personnel manager is to develop a vision of what might be, he or she must have some sense of being able to make choices in their work.

Integrating with the business

An effective personnel strategy clearly needs to be as closely aligned to the business as possible. The degree of alignment may vary:

1. It may be fully integrated at the primary level of strategy formulation. Here personnel strategy is so closely allied to the overall business strategy that it is in effect totally merged with it. In other

words, the HR issue is so crucial that the business plan depends on it; in fact, the business plan may even have been determined by people considerations.

2. Personnel strategy is fully integrated but at a secondary level of strategy formulation. In other words, the overall business strategy is decided, and then the personnel implications follow. (Some have argued that this is bound to be so, given that personnel strategy relates to functional issues which are by definition at this secondary level. The whole thrust of this book is that this is selling ourselves short.)

3. Here, personnel strategy is not integrated with any formal business plan but is very much business oriented. This is likely to reflect a situation where no well defined business plan is in place. Being realistic, one has to recognise that this is often the case. Despite this, the personnel manager can still plan strategic action, providing it is based on a first class understanding of the business.

4. The fourth possibility is a personnel strategy which is not integrated with any formal business plan and is essentially personnel rather than business oriented. In other words, a strategy primarily focused on 'best practice'. The danger is that it takes on a life of its own, running on maybe parallel but separate tracks from the business. Until relatively recently, this was perhaps an acceptable approach, despite its obvious limitations. Today, it is the modern equivalent of falling heroically, but fatally, on one's sword!

The questions

Here is a series of questions enabling you to identify where your strategic opportunities may lie.

Does the organisation have a mission statement? If yes, what are the people implications?

A certain group of restaurants are currently displaying a notice in each establishment – 'The Group now has a *mission statement* – to be the best restaurant group in the UK'. Whether this is a realistic mission or not is beside the point. What is clear is that such a mission has profound implications for the way the group manages its people and for the role of personnel. First and foremost it will be essential for the company to recruit people with the right aptitude for service and the capacity to learn the relevant catering skills. It will be vital to retain such people and train them effectively. Pay will be a sensitive issue – competitive, felt to be fair and reward performance, without pushing costs through the roof. Unless these people objectives are achieved, the company has no hope of achieving its mission.

Does the organisation have a set of strategic objectives? If yes, what are the people implications?

J. Sainsbury, the leading grocers, signalled some years ago its objective to diversify into other retailing areas, such as DIY. Again the people implications were profound: for example, for management development. Can it be assumed that retailing skills are common for the different businesses? To what extent would it be necessary to recruit senior managers from outside? What impact would the relative slowdown in growth in the traditional grocery sector have on career development within the group?

In what ways does your function directly impact on the organisation's customers and/or suppliers?

A leading health-care company, Western Provident, identified that the way it dealt with customers and potential customers was a critical aspect of winning competitive advantage. This had implications not only for immediate sales staff, but for people throughout the firm, whether dealing with telephone enquiries, preparing policies, responding to queries, or dealing with claims. It decided that the Investors in People Award would provide an appropriate framework for its training and development policies, and in fact recognition has been achieved.

Name two significant problems which the organisation has, where your function could contribute to a solution

In the mid-'80s, one firm was being held back by a relationship with its recognised trade unions based on a history of conflict. Strategically, the personnel function defined its task as not merely to resolve difficulties as they arose, but to change the whole nature of the relationship. Today, the organisation and the trade unions concerned have established a constructive level of collaboration, and indeed partnership, which has played a major part in facilitating strategic change.

Suggest two other ways in which your function could contribute to strategic improvement

The personnel function has to be constantly on the look-out for new ways to move the business forward. Van den Bergh Foods saw just such a chance when the concept of profit-related pay came on to the statute book. Some 2000 employees now benefit from their approved scheme. Their employee development manager is quoted as saying:

> Profit-Related Pay has had a useful part to play in our strategic approach to change management. Convincing people of the need to work differently and then pointing to the benefits on the bottom line – which they can experience through tax free payments and bonuses – has been the main achievement.

What are the obstacles which are currently inhibiting you from improving your contribution to your organisation?

At the beginning of this chapter, we noted the kind of obstacles faced by many personnel managers who seek to move down the strategic road. There is no doubt that these are very real in many organisations. Tackling them is a process of systematic problem solving:

1.   Clearly define the problem. (The real problem is often different from what appears on the surface. At the heart of many problems are relationship issues.)
2.   Work out various options, and the advantages and disadvantages of each.
3.   Decide on the preferred solution and start working on it.

Of course, obstacles will often be deep-seated and the problem-solving approach may seem simplistic. Yet once you start on the process, providing it is done in a thorough way, solutions – or at least improvements – will start to present themselves.

Are there any relationships within the organisation causing you particular difficulty?

There almost invariably will be, if this question is answered honestly! It is important to face up to such difficulties and deal with them. The solution will be at one of these levels:

● *The problem is resolved* Whatever it was that caused some breakdown in the relationship is removed; perhaps a long standing misunderstanding is talked through or perhaps relative roles become better understood.

- *The problem is mitigated* It will not always be possible to resolve relationship issues fully, especially if they stem from a genuine personality clash. A state of, as it were, mutual sufferance may be the most that can be achieved.
- *The problem is bypassed* Some personal relationships will never work. If so, it is best to recognise that in such cases it is a matter of ongoing damage limitation. It is wise to be doubly sure to provide good service to a colleague who is not predisposed to be friendly – a technique known as ensuring you are 'bomb proof'!

Let us be frank about something which is not always tackled in books on personnel management. *The personnel function cannot escape issues of power and politics.* Because we are dealing with people, these are inevitable in any organisation.

In this context, there are two golden rules which all personnel people must clearly understand. First, where you have a problem with someone it is essential to deal with it face to face – especially where the personnel department has made a mistake. Secondly, bullies must be stood up to. Those who are aggressive towards personnel people will only be checked if you make a stand.

In short, the effective personnel manager has to be 'street-wise'.

At the moment, what is your single biggest challenge?

If this turns out to be something of a purely operational or administrative nature, it is a sure sign that you have not spotted your strategic opportunities.

What is the next step in your personal development?

Moving your role or function or department down the strategic road has personal ramifications. Continuous improvement for the one implies continuing personal development for the other. This must be included in your strategic plan.

THE MODEL PHASE 3: THE PERSONNEL FUNCTION AS A BUSINESS

We turn now to the third element in our model – looking at the function as a business. Thinking in these terms reorientates our focus from the administrative typically 'personnel' type of agenda to a genuinely business oriented one.

This part of the model suggests four questions.

Who are your clients?

We have already looked at this issue in Chapter 4.

What is your mission?

It is worth spending some time working out a distinctive mission statement for the function. The process of doing so presents interesting team-building opportunities. It could well be appropriate to bring the personnel team together to thrash out such a statement. Perhaps some allies among line management could join the exercise. Certainly, once a draft statement has emerged it would be important to test out the draft among line colleagues. Normally, the definitive statement needs to have the real support of senior management.

One such mission statement reads as follows:

> We work for a business whose only real assets are its people. The mission of the personnel function is to bring to bear professional services and expertise, based on a sound understanding of the business, such that the organisation has the capability to produce consistently superior results. It is also part of our mission to enable all employees to perform to the best of their ability.

Do you have adequate resources?

The strategic personnel manager will be clear what resources the function needs in well thought out and articulated business terms. He or she will have a total 'handle' on how current resources are deployed and how much they cost. Some business ratios to help do this are scheduled in Table 6.1.

All functions within a business have to fight their corner for resources. There are many pointers in this book to help personnel do as good a job on this as any other function.

Table 6.1 *Business ratios for personnel*

- Ratio of HR/personnel staff to number of employees (full time equivalents)
- Ratio of managerial/professional personnel staff to number of employees
- Salaries and bonus of HR/personnel department as per cent of organisation salaries and bonus
- Salary and bonus cost of HR/personnel department per employee
- Direct staff costs of HR/personnel department as per cent of the total organisation direct staff costs
- Indirect costs of the HR/personnel department as per cent of total organisation indirect costs
- Total recruitment costs per new recruit
- Overall training cost per employee

Source: with acknowledgement to MCP Management Consultants of John Street, London WC1.

What are your plans for your personal development, and those of your people, over the next 24 months? how will you win support for these?

Robust employee development plans are essential for any business. This must include the personnel function. There is only one way to win support for such training and development plans, and that is to demonstrate the business case for them. Would your own function be recognised as an 'investor in people'?

A final question

Do you have well defined priorities, goals and performance criteria?

If you have worked systematically through the model set out here, you will be in an excellent position to write down a winning business plan for your function.

Key questions

- What were the most pertinent aspects of this chapter for you?
- In the spirit of continuous improvement, what parts of the model need the most work over the next two years, as far as you are concerned?
- Do you have an effective way to review progress?

Notes

1. With acknowledgment to MCP Management Consultants.

7

Task – The New Agenda for Personnel

"Our ability to build and make accessible the comprehensive body
of knowledge which underpins our profession will be key to
the effectiveness of our members and of the new institute".
Geoff Armstrong, Director General, Institute of Personnel and Development

WHAT IS THE NEW AGENDA?

There is profound ignorance among the general public about the role
and activities of the personnel function. In fact all too often this extends
to the state of knowledge on the subject within organisations. There is a
vague idea that it is to do with recruitment and perhaps helping people
in trouble. No doubt one reason for this is that, as mentioned in the
previous chapter, many personnel people are notoriously weak in public
relations. However, another reason is that many managers regard
supervising others as a matter of 'common sense'. The fact that many of
them are fairly bad at it seems to escape their attention. As the old adage
has it, the problem with common sense is that it ain't that common.

In any case, it is *not* a matter of common sense. As Armstrong goes on
to say[1] 'it is a systematic learnable discipline, with a wide range of
explicit competencies'. An important feature for the individual intent on
developing the more strategic approach is that he or she must have a first
class grasp of these competencies.

The challenge of the changing agenda

Moreover the agenda is changing. In referring to practices applying to the employment relationship, Tyson of Cranfield writes[2] that, in the light of dramatic change, companies will have in future to think of different kinds of practices to apply to the employment relationship. 'What we are witnessing are different strategic responses to the new environments of the 1990s.' His conclusion is highly relevant to the contentions in this book:

> The structural changes brought about by the recession are irreversible: Personnel professionals have found themselves in a different position from the one envisioned by optimistic commentators in the mid 1980s. By concentrating on change management in the cold economic climate of the 1990s they are expected to be business-led, cost conscious and flexible.
>
> However, this does presage a more mature future – the possibility of total integration between human resource and business strategy to the benefit of customers and the economy as a whole.

Yet if this future is to be realised, the function has to address itself to the new agenda, and avoid clinging to the traditional comfortable activities of the past. There are a number of studies which provide clues as to the content of this new agenda.

The Cranfield findings

The authors of the Cranfield study found three substantive areas where all the companies researched typically used human resource management to play a strategic role: employee and management development, employee relations strategies and organisation development.

The Personnel Standards Lead Body (PSLB)

As part of its work, the Personnel Standards Lead Body (PSLB) surveyed close to 1000 senior personnel practitioners to establish areas where there was scope for improvement in the level of competence demonstrated by the personnel function. Areas perceived to be of high importance to organisational success but which were not being tackled effectively included:

● promote effective communication within the organisation
● establishing and maintaining performance management processes
● establishing opportunities to enhance individual capabilities
● promoting longer term individual and team development processes

- identifying individual potential to develop and meet future resourcing requirements

On the other hand, subjects which were perceived to be handled best were the more traditional areas of recruitment, pay and benefits administration, joint consultation and grievance and discipline procedures.

'Winning people'

To some degree, the thrust of this thinking was confirmed by a third piece of work, the study by the London Human Resource Group (LHRG), entitled *Winning People*. This contended that the firms studied had successfully tackled the direct issues of restructuring and cost-cutting, but had a long way to go in the more difficult areas of developing staff for the new era and winning their real commitment.

European Association of Personnel Management (EAPM)

Yet another study, that of the European Association of Personnel Management (EAPM) *The Emerging Role of the HR Manager in Europe*, identified management development, organisation development and strategic HR planning as the subjects of most importance for the future. Of a substantial list of topics, least important were personnel administration and old style industrial relations.

The 1991 IBM study

Finally, we turn to the IBM worldwide human resource study conducted by Towers Perrin, *Priorities for Competitive Advantage: a 21st century vision*. The questionnaire identified 23 human resource activities, and respondents were asked to judge future priorities. The activities rated above 70 per cent were:

- workforce productivity/quality
- management/executive development
- teamwork
- workforce planning
- employee education and training
- employee and manager communications.

UK respondents added 'succession and development planning' to this list. Building on this, survey participants ranked the top five initiatives for competitive advantage as:

- communicate directions, plans, problems
- reward customer service and quality
- identify high-potential employees early
- reward innovation and creativity
- reward business and/or productivity gains.

UK respondents substituted 'emphasise management development/skills training' in their top five, rather than 'reward innovation and creativity'.

A MODEL FOR THE NEW STRATEGIC AGENDA

Let's try to draw these threads together to set out a model of the new strategic agenda (see Figure 7.1). First and foremost, people are employed to deliver a product or service to the customer, so 'performance management' is the key to the model – the way the task is managed. Personnel strategy has a direct role to play in the delivery of high performance.

Secondly comes 'organisation structure and development': the way individuals are deployed. This is linked to the third element, 'employee development': the way individuals at all levels are trained and developed for the tasks in hand.

The final element is the environment within which all these activities take place: in other words, 'employee relations' issues.

The importance of holistic thinking

One of the difficulties in trying to draw up a definitive model of this new agenda is that so many aspects are interlinked. For example, performance related pay is primarily seen as an inherent part of performance management. Yet one of the criticisms it has faced as a technique is that it pays insufficient regard to the issue of teamworking. In many companies it also has a developmental role, and in yet other cases it has a profound impact on the employee relations environment. In other words it is inextricably linked to all three of the elements listed above.

In terms of the way the personnel function is organised, there is here a clear analogy with the principles of re-engineering. Personnel initiatives

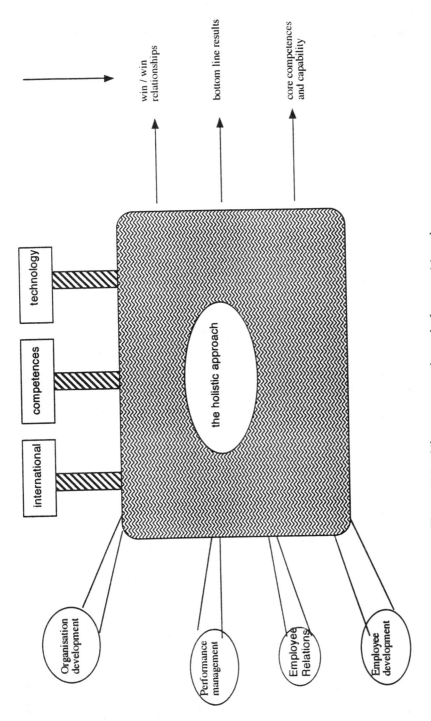

Figure 7.1   *The new personnel agenda for competitive advantage*

have to be regarded in a holistic way and can no longer be delivered in specialist isolation. Performance related pay (PRP) has often failed because of a failure to pay heed to this strategic principle.

This has obvious implications for the development of personnel professionals.

Linking themes

In following up the point that these functions need to be looked at holistically, one becomes aware of a number of themes linking them. The first of these is the theme of 'competences', which some companies have used as the determining feature of human resource strategy as a whole. Secondly, one cannot ignore the importance of 'technology', the technical means of delivering many of these services in the best possible way. Thirdly, in these days of global markets, it is essential to keep well in mind the 'international' dimension.

The extent of personnel involvement

The role and influence of the personnel function in any one of these areas varies enormously from one firm to another. If you wish to increase your level of involvement – in other words, to go further down the strategic road – you need to analyse where you are currently. A helpful way of looking at this is as follows:

- *Level 1 – administrative* Personnel simply administers a system according to management's requirements, with no influence on its design or interest in its performance or contribution to business need.
- *Level 2 – operational* Personnel manages a system or function in operational terms and is accountable for operational results, but without any input as to its strategic importance or contribution.
- *Level 3 – strategy implementation* Personnel has responsibility for implementing strategic decisions but no involvement in the strategic decision-making process.
- *Level 4 – strategy formulation* Personnel has a clear role in the strategic decision-making process.

It is quite feasible that the personnel function may operate at different levels for different aspects of the strategic agenda. For example, the personnel manager may be regarded as expert in the employee relations field, and may be looked to for advice on strategy formulation in that field, ie at level 4, while operating only at level 2 when it comes to, say, executive remuneration.

The second half of this chapter looks more closely at each item on the new agenda, and points in a practical way to some of their key features. As we move through the agenda, you may well wish to discern the level at which you are currently operating. Is this the appropriate level for you? Going further down the strategic road will almost certainly mean making a plan to raise the level in certain areas. If, to take the above example, you are indeed only at level 2 for executive remuneration – which is often the case – what practical steps are open to you to start raising your sights at least to level 3?

TACKLING THE NEW AGENDA

It is not the purpose of this book to cover in textbook detail the various functions of personnel management. What matters in our context is to point up some of the strategic aspects of this new agenda, particularly by the use of practical examples.

PERFORMANCE MANAGEMENT

We have already said that performance management lies at the heart of the new agenda. It provides a clear opportunity to demonstrate the contribution of personnel expertise to the bottom line. Yet if personnel practitioners are to be really effective in this arena, they must be able to combine real knowledge and understanding of the complex ramifications of the subject with the business acumen and cultural sensitivity necessary to implement performance management processes in their own environment.

And the relationship with pay

A key, and controversial, issue is the relationship between performance and pay. As far as many managements are concerned, the start point down the road to enhanced performance is the pay system. This is hardly surprising, given the touching faith – not to say prejudice – of so many managers in a direct link between pay and performance. In fact the evidence for positive links between pay and performance is patchy, to say the least.

Findings from Templeton

A recent research project on performance related pay (PRP) conducted by Kessler and Purcell of Templeton College, Oxford,[3] concluded that 'the difficulties of measuring the impact of a pay system, or indeed any other personnel system, on individual and organisational behaviour are notorious'. Nevertheless, they reported that within two companies where they were able to conduct attitude surveys directly related to the introduction of PRP, the principle commanded strong support.

The researchers identified three dilemmas or choices for managers:

- *Cultural break or cultural sensitivity* PRP may be used as a deliberate attempt to break with the past: what the researchers described as 'the creation of pressure points forcing change'. In other cases, it was felt important to remain sensitive to existing norms so as to facilitate the acceptance of change and to avoid undue conflict.
- *PRP as follower or leader* Should PRP be seen as the main engine of change, or should it play a supportive role? The former was the case in one of the organisations studied, British Rail, while in Amersham International it was seen as 'the last piece of the jigsaw'.
- *Developing management skills* The researchers found a real dilemma here. Sometimes PRP was intended to encourage the development of management skills, yet problems were faced in implementation just because managers lacked the skills to operate the scheme in the first place.

These are just the kind of issues where management should be able to look for personnel expertise and judgment. Indeed, Kessler and Purcell point to one of the real personnel challenges:

> There was a danger that the problems arising in the learning stage of a scheme might discredit it in the eyes of employees before it became fully accepted. Personnel departments sometimes compensated for line management difficulties by playing a highly intrusive role, issuing guidelines and closely monitoring schemes. This, in turn, risked line manager resentment at the intrusiveness of the personnel department.

And from the IMS

The headline finding of another research project, this time conducted by the Institute of Manpower Studies (IMS), was quite specific: 'Performance pay is not a motivator'. The analysis of schemes in three organisations concluded that 'there is little evidence to show that PRP helps retain high performers or encourages poor performers to leave'. Nevertheless, 'employees who have been involved in the design and implementation of a scheme are more likely to perceive it as being fair and to be motivated'.[4]

This is not a message that will come as a huge surprise to personnel practitioners, and underlines once again the input needed from the function in this field. It illustrates the model set out above concerning the degree of personnel involvement. If the IMS study is right, personnel must get involved at least at level 3 (strategy implementation) so that the new scheme is conceived and implemented along the right lines.

The importance of approaching these matters from a strategic viewpoint and on a basis of real expertise is underlined by a number of surveys whose findings indicate that many organisations introducing PRP have found it counter-productive. The tendency has been to see a new pay system, with its attendant use of performance appraisal and objective setting, as an end in itself rather than as an element in encouraging individual and corporate performance long term.

The challenge of teamworking

A particular aspect of the problem has been highlighted by Murlis and others, namely the challenge of performance management and reward in the team context – 'recognising and paying for team performance, with all its appeal of reinforcing co-operation and collaboration and avoiding the divisiveness of individual performance related pay'.[5] Much criticism of PRP stems from its failure to take account of team needs. Given the new focus on teamworking, often resulting from a re-engineering exercise, this seems highly pertinent.

Yet in practice, the right balance between individual and team has often proved elusive. Some schemes have foundered on the troublesome issue of how to deal with underperformance of individuals within the team. Those who are really achieving and contributing most to the team wish naturally enough to be recognised and not to be held back by the weaker performers.

Murlis points out that it is critical to identify different types of teamworking and to design pay architecture accordingly. She defines five main kinds of teams:

- the ad hoc task force
- the partnership

- the multiskilled project team
- the product/service work team
- the task team working together, but as individuals.

Teamworking in the Automobile Association

The particular characteristic of the Automobile Association (AA) is that service is delivered to the customer by the individual patrolperson, yet patrols are organised in teams including emergency telephone operators and mechanics. It was recognised that the incentive system encouraged speed of working at the roadside, sometimes to the detriment of quality to the customer and a real sense of teamworking. A new system was introduced, known as 'Teamwork pays'. This rewarded staff on two basic criteria, the overall performance of the organisation, and a set of local performance measures on which teams compete in leagues. Reward includes money, but is also based on recognition; among other things, there is a 'Patrol team of the year' award, where members receive a gift and there is an event such as a night out for everyone and their families.[6]

Performance management and customer service

The AA system focuses strongly on the customer. One consultancy, Oxford Training, produced a set of criteria for effective PRP schemes and it is significant that the first criterion links PRP with quality and customer service (see Table 7.1).

Eastern Electricity

One company which took this very much to heart was Eastern Electricity.[7] In 1993/4, they introduced a pay system based entirely on performance. The first issue that they faced was to ensure that all employees were clear about what they were expected to do, and what performance meant for them. This led rapidly to a process whereby work teams identified their customers, whether internal or external, and specified the needs of those customers. As the staff development manager wrote:

> ... this enables people to focus on their ultimate purpose, which must always be to provide a service to others. By agreeing how their customers will measure their effectiveness, teams begin to be clearer about what sort of things they need to do collectively and individually to be successful.

Table 7.1

Effective PRP	Poor PRP
Effective PRP schemes are based on the assumption that, given the opportunity, people at work want to do a good job, serving internal and external customers with quality goods and services. PRP is introduced because of its fairness.	Poor PRP schemes are based on the assumption that people at work do not want to do a good job, and must therefore be bribed to increase their efforts through the offer of extra cash.
Effective PRP schemes focus on what people have contributed to the team and organisation. Formal, written objectives are used as one of the means to communicate to people what's required, but it's acknowledged that in times of rapid change it's overall contribution that really matters.	Poor PRP schemes use objectives, not as a communication and planning tool to improve performance, but as an examination through which to assess pay. Objectives therefore come to be seen not as things with relevance to real, operational needs, but as an administrative ritual to determine pay.
In good PRP schemes managers are trained to make assessments of performance and contribution, using a language of behavioural competency. The techniques are used, first and foremost, to provide people with feedback and coaching. But their use means that, when it comes to the time for pay review, assessments are made on the basis of hard evidence, understood and trusted by those under review.	Poor PRP schemes provide no training to managers in how to assess performance; unsurprisingly, those being assessed fear favouritism and patronage.
Effective PRP systems ensure consistency of judgments across departments by providing a forum in which managers making assessments cross-check and validate their judgments by testing their decisions against those of their colleagues, jointly examining the evidence to support them.	Poor PRP schemes allow for no such checks, reinforcing the suspicion that judgments may be arbitrary and unfair.

Source: Reproduced by permission of Oxford Training, of Long Harborough, Oxfordshire

Predictably, this has often resulted in an agreed action to do some urgent customer research!.

Like many companies, Eastern Electricity found that the use of appraisal had been patchy, to say the least. This had to be remedied and the first step was to develop an Appraisal Charter:

As an employee of Eastern Electricity you can expect your appraisal to be handled in a fair and consistent way. Specifically, you can expect the following

- At the beginning of the performance period you will have the opportunity to discuss your performance with your boss and agree your objectives in the coming year.
- At the same time, a Personal Development Plan will be agreed between you and your boss.
- Your boss will handle your appraisal fairly and professionally and in accordance with our Equal Opportunities Policy. You will get regular feedback on your performance with a formal review after 6 months.
- You will be encouraged to appraise your own performance.
- Your objectives will conform to the ASTREAM criteria ie they will be: Agreed, Specific, Time bounded, Relevant, Empowering, Achievable, and Measurable. If you are dissatisfied with the process at any stage, you have the right to ask for your boss's boss to be present in the discussions.

This approach clearly links appraisal, performance and personal development. The performance management cycle is set out in Figure 7.2. Some of the key features of this cycle are as follows:

- *Recognition of the importance of the team* Work teams are involved in developing their own key performance areas (KPAs), and individual objectives are derived from these KPAs.
- *Objectives agreed, not imposed* This is constantly stressed. Individuals begin to establish their own objectives before discussing them with their boss.
- *Encourages a coaching approach* The manager's coaching role is emphasised, and specifically built into the cycle.

The case of Bass

In another case, that of brewers Bass plc, the concern of the HR director was how to make HR strategies business-led. One part of the answer was to introduce programmes aimed at enhancing corporate capability.

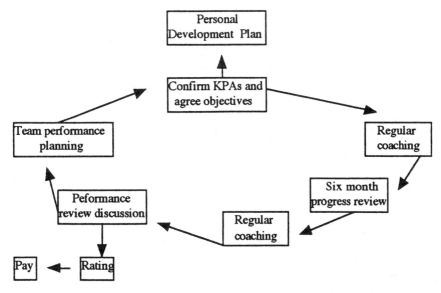

Source: Reproduced by kind permission of Oxford Training

Figure 7.2   *Eastern Electricity's performance management cycle*

Corporate capability was defined as the ability of the company to identify, plan and successfully implement change. The areas of change included strategy, policy, structure, competitive tactics and technological and product innovation. The effectiveness of each programme had to be measured through linkage to measures of corporate performance. Interestingly, the function determined that speed of response was as important as the quality of that response.

Another important element was the determination to work as closely as possible with line management. All aspects of the approach to performance management were subject to clearly defined and understood ways of working together, the various players being the employee, the line boss, the HR function and the board. For example, four determinants of the reward package were identified – the value of the person, job size, market value of the job, and company norms (ie the ability to pay). The matrix in Table 7.2 shows the role of each player. In this case, line management has substantial ownership of the process, without detracting in any way from the value of the HR contribution.

Performance management in a manufacturing context

I noted earlier, that people issues are intrinsic to any attempt to improve

Table 7.2

	Employee	Line boss	HR function	Board
Value of the person	**	**		
Job size		**	**	
Market value			**	**
Company norm			**	**

productivity. Modern production methods have moved from the batch production model to so-called lean production. This brings human resource management to the fore. Whereas under batch production the emphasis in terms of personnel management is on policies and procedures, in a lean production environment the emphasis is on a more dynamic approach, building inter-team working where each team and every individual is highly dependent on the others' efforts. Here again, a coaching approach is fundamental, combined with continuous learning and development.

ORGANISATION DEVELOPMENT

I have already referred at various points in this book to the new demands on business, with all that this implies for the way organisations are structured and managed. One way of looking at this was set out in a model developed by consultants, Kinsley Lord, encapsulating much of what organisation development now involves (see Table 7.3).[8] The managerial task is moving rapidly from the old 'command and control' to the enabling coaching role. The insights and expertise of the personnel function make it a key player in ensuring that this transition achieves positive and lasting results.

An example from the chemical industry

The chemicals manufacturer, Hickson Fine Chemicals, switched to a system of teamworking as part of a drive to engage the whole workforce in a process of continuous improvement.[9] This represented a considerable challenge to a company that by its own admission had been based for many years on a traditional hierarchical form of organisation. The aim was to help people work effectively rather than to police and control them.

Table 7.3   *Building an empowered organisation*

From the command organisation	To the empowered organisation
Remote top management, concerned with strategic planning, management control, external relations	Visible top management, providing a vision of the future which employees understand and share
Middle management mainly about control, direction, and downward communication	Middle management mainly about inspiring and encouraging people and enabling change
Individuals told what to do, with jobs defined as sets of tasks	Teams 'contract' their contribution to the organisation, with jobs defined in terms of team role
Status comes from job grade and place in the pecking order	Status comes from contribution to the organisation
Thinking is up and down the organisation, in functional 'drainpipes'	Thinking is across the organisation, in cross-functional project groups and informal teams
People stop learning	People keep learning
Energy is low	Energy is high

Source: Reproduced by permission of Kinsey Lord Management Consultants of Old Queen Street, London SW1, 1991.

The new approach has had a particular impact on the role of supervisors, now called team leaders. The new team leaders have accepted responsibility for larger groups of people and wider geographical areas within the plant. Many day-to-day tasks previously the prerogative of plant managers have been delegated to the team leaders, leaving managers freer to concentrate on wider aspects of the business. Meanwhile, the prime task of the team leaders is motivating and bringing the best out of those they lead.

And from insurance

This kind of development is by no means confined to manufacturing. A very different sort of firm, the Sun Life Assurance Society, set out to redesign its core business processes from scratch.[10] The lesson drawn from their experience is that the technical aspects of process re-engineering are only half the story. Just as critical was enabling people to contribute personally within new customer-focused teams.

Clerks became front-line people, entitled case managers, with full accountability for seeing a case through its full process, and dealing directly with the client. Their managers moved from being primarily policy experts to enablers of others, whose performance was now measured less on technical expertise, and more on how successful they were in motivating others to deliver first class customer service.

Another leading insurance company is seeking its own route to corporate transformation, where once again the personnel function has a leading role. A conference of senior managers spent time analysing the company's source of competitive advantage, now and in the future. One of their most important conclusions was surprising on the face of it, but promises to have dynamic results over time. They were clear that only those firms with excellent quality and service would survive, but what would distinguish the winner from among this already leading group?

Their response was – *the quality of thinking at all levels of the organisation.* It was this which would produce the truly innovative solutions to client problems and enable the organisation to achieve true flexibility and responsiveness. This vision is leading to a whole series of initiatives, shared by both the line and personnel.

EMPLOYEE DEVELOPMENT

The new personnel agenda closely links organisational development with the development of the individual employee. In the Hickson case for example, management recognised that the development of team leaders had to be regarded on an individual as well as a group basis, reflecting individual strengths and weaknesses.

A commonality of interest?

It is also in this field that one can see most clearly the commonality of interest between the needs of the individual employee and those of the employer. In his publication, *Managing Careers: Strategies for Organisations*, Andrew Mayo defined career management as 'the design and implementation of processes that enable the careers of individuals to be planned and managed in a way that optimises both the needs of the organisation and the preferences of the individual'.

While this sounds like a truism, in many instances it is ignored by employers. For example, the London Human Resource Group *Winning People* report found that few organisations had matched their rhetoric about employability replacing 'job for life' security. 'Current efforts by employers [to promote employability and empowerment] are perceived by middle managers and staff as a one-sided deal.' The report found that from 40 per cent to 65 per cent of staff would consider changing their job if the opportunity arose.

A survey of 123 personnel directors conducted by MORI and consultants Strategic People found that 70 per cent were cutting jobs and 42 per cent were reducing the number of grades. On the other hand, fewer than half had developed any kind of policy to motivate and develop managers in a de-layered organisation. Yet, as another consultant put it:

> ... individuals want to make use of the full range of their skills and talents and to express themselves in what they do. If this is not achieved in an organisation setting, other outlets are found at home, at leisure or in smaller organisations which have re-invented the rules for working arrangements and lifestyles.

One might add – to the detriment of the employing organisations. It is perhaps not surprising that increasing numbers of people seem to have as their main ambition to reach retirement.

The Christian Salvesen initiative

These issues were taken on board by shipping group Christian Salvesen, when it realised that its previous approaches to career development had become outmoded.[11] It had accordingly abandoned detailed career planning based on moving up the organisation in favour of developing the individual's unique career. HR head Richard Coles stated:

> ... the leaner, flatter organisation will result in people developing their contribution without any apparent career steps. Careers will consist of employees continually evolving while apparently remaining in the same job.

He gave the caveat that this will not just happen: 'it has to be worked at'.

Easier said than done

For some organisations such a vision of employee development implies radical changes of attitude. At a recent seminar, someone commented that her ambition was to continue to work hard for five years, and then to move down to the West Country to open a pub with her husband. She was asked whether she had shared this planning with her boss. Certainly not, was the response, he would think it was disloyal.

An employee development map for the '90s

If we were to draw a map to help us to cover the ground in the employee development field, what might it look like?

It would start with some of the drivers creating development/learning needs (see Figure 7.3), and it would include generic learning needs derived from such drivers (see Figure 7.4). Finally, the map would enable us to explore issues around the delivery of training and development (see Figure 7.5). The map would home in on these issues more closely than is appropriate in this brief review of the new personnel agenda. Two aspects however need further attention, because they highlight opportunities for a real contribution from the personnel and training functions.

● *external business pressures*

eg service and quality
   technology
   competition and costs

● *other external pressures*

eg social change
   legislative
   public accountability
   rise of the knowledge worker

● *business responses*

eg flatter structures
   empowerment
   devolution from personnel to the line
     cost cutting
   lean production/JIT/re-engineering

Figure 7.3   *Employee development map: drivers*

● *attitudes*

eg dealing with ambiguity
   taking personal initiative
   self-confidence

● *personal effectiveness*

eg technical competence
   capacity to learn
   problem-solving
   organising skills

● *dealing with others*

eg coaching
   enabling
   communication skills
   negotiating skills
   personnel skills

Figure 7.4   *Employee development map: needs*

● *the adult learning process*

eg learning style preferences
   learning on the job
   the manager as coach
   accelerated learning

● *the learning environment*

eg the learning organisation
   external frameworks – NVQs,
   modern apprenticeship,
   continuous professional
   development

● *measurement and review*

eg setting objectives for training
   new approaches to appraisal
   the link with business needs

Figure 7.5   *Employee development map: training*

First, the learning organisation

Training and development will not flourish unless the environment within an organisation is conducive to it. Here is a list of factors which characterise a true 'learning organisation':

- values and mission statements set the 'climate' for learning
- these are reflected in the behaviour of senior executives
- the organisation has learning goals and measures against them
- key impact of remuneration policy is taken fully into account
- individuals are encouraged to take responsibility for their own learning
- organisation provides opportunities for staff to improve employability
- employee surveys and benchmarking major on learning opportunities
- policy and practice conforms to national standards, such as NVQs, Investors in People (IIP).

Second, the importance of an integrated learning approach

An integrated approach means that training and development take account of all the factors which encourage or inhibit effective learning. It is helpful to see this in terms of a force field analysis and one model for such an analysis is shown in Figure 7.6. In this illustration, the development identified is improved teamworking, and there are forces pushing for this improvement in terms of business needs. The traditional response is to look at skill needs and arrange training to remedy them. Often the training proves to be relatively ineffective, because the

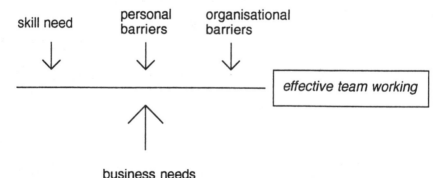

Figure 7.6   *A force field analysis for integrated learning*

other negative forces – personal and organisational barriers – are ignored. The desired improvement will not take place unless these other forces are also tackled; in other words, an integrated approach to the required learning.

The problem is that these other barriers are more subtle and less tractable than the more straightforward matter of defining the skills involved.

The personal barriers

Let us look briefly at some of the personal barriers. Any learning has to enable the individual to move through certain stages before durable changes in behaviour take place. The first stage is *awareness*. Individuals need to become aware of their skill deficiency – in effect incompetence. For example, many managers are poor at handling others because they are quite simply unaware of the skills involved. In other words, they are in a state of 'unconscious incompetence'.

The second stage is *understanding*. The trainee needs to understand what the skill involves in terms of practical action. For example, it is little use getting an individual to become aware that he or she is a poor communicator without also helping him or her to grasp in detail what the skills involved really are – for example, active listening. We need to move the trainee to a state of 'conscious incompetence'.

The third stage is *commitment*. This is usually the most difficult stage. Does the trainee really want to change in their heart of hearts? What's in it for them? Is there an acceptance that, say, being an effective team player really matters in practice? It may well involve a quite painful process of unlearning. Reflecting on the last decade, one notes a huge range of workers who have had to unlearn in order to move in often unwanted new directions, ranging from GPs taking on budgetary responsibilities, to care workers having to move out into the community, to brokers having to take managerial skills on board, to production workers taking responsibility for their own quality – the list is legion.

Accepting commitment to new learning involves moving to 'conscious competence', the process whereby one reviews one's own progress towards acquiring the new skill. It is only when these processes are complete that one may be confident that there has been a sustainable *behaviour change*; in other words, when the new skill has become truly part of the individual's kitbag and is exercised in a way that is 'unconsciously competent'.

The organisational barriers

Even then, the new skills are not practised wholeheartedly in many cases because they are discouraged by the organisational environment. If for example, professional expertise is clearly more highly valued than managerial skills by the powers that be in an organisation, it is unlikely that middle-ranking professionals will do more than pay lip service to them. Again, if senior managers react to developmental activities in a grudging way, making clear that they regard them as a waste of time dreamt up by personnel – well, personnel will have a hard time!

Example of excellence – the Rover Group

One firm that has established some unique approaches to this challenge is the Rover Group. Not only has the company established 'corporate learning' as one of its prime business processes, but it has set up a separate organisation to develop the process, Rover Learning Business. This has its own board and executive committee, responsible for providing all employees with excellent training and development opportunities. At its inception, it received the personal endorsement of the then chairman, Sir Graham Day.

To summarise the strategic role in employee development

The personnel function will not be performing in a strategic way if it is simply a provider of training events, however excellent in themselves. Over and beyond that, it needs to:

- identify those development needs which are essential to support business goals and objectives and to secure employee commitment to the organisation
- nurture an environment conducive to effective learning, including the thorough and genuine involvement of line management
- deliver appropriate development processes
- ensure that the organisation regularly reviews and updates its development policies and programmes.

EMPLOYEE RELATIONS

The third element of the new agenda is the employee relations environment. This is on the new agenda not only because of its intrinsic importance as part of HR strategy but because there has been such a fundamental shift in thinking and practice. Purcell and Ahlstrand illustrated this in their book *Human Resource Management in the Multi-Divisional Company* (Figure 7.7).[12]

INDIVIDUALISM	RESOURCE			
		Sophisticated human relations		Sophisticated consultative
		Paternalist		Modern paternalist
	COMMODITY	Traditional	Bargained constitutional	??
		None (Unitary)	Adversarial	Cooperative
			COLLECTIVISM	

Source: Purcell and Ahlstrand 1994. Reproduced by permission of Oxford University Press

Figure 7.7 *Employee relations environments*

Purcell and Ahlstrand make the not unreasonable assumption that it is not a viable proposition for a company to remain stuck in the old adversarial 'bargained constitutional' mode. The challenge and opportunity for personnel practitioners is to define the new mode that will be most appropriate for the organisation and to play a leading role in helping to navigate a path to that strategic goal.

Given the current emphasis on individualism, the obvious route might seem to be to the 'sophisticated human relations' mode. Here employees are encouraged to sign new individual contracts and union recognition is withdrawn. It seems to open the way to new work practices and a new focus on employee development and performance management. It has been a route favoured by a number of corporations, particularly in the United States. It may well be the right way for some to go.

But it is not *necessarily* the right way to go, seductive as it may seem at first sight. Here are some other factors:

1. It removes what can be, handled correctly, an important channel of dialogue with employees as a whole. Once individualised, real employee concerns may not reach through the hierarchy to decision-makers. Processes of change may become more difficult to manage.
2. It may be problematic to sustain this mode under pressure. Should economic circumstances become less favourable, it may prove necessary to move down to a more traditional cost minimisation mode. As Purcell points out, once that move has been implemented it may be difficult to escape from it.
3. A change of political climate may impose some kind of collective rules, as for example following the European Works Council Directive.
4. According to the third workplace industrial relations survey (1990),[13] positive employee development practices were more prevalent in unionised workplaces. Some of the findings of the survey were:
    *   multiple channels of communication were more likely to be used in unionised workplaces
    *   non-union workplaces were characterised by authoritarian and hierarchical management practices
    *   non-unionised workers had few opportunities to influence their working lives
    *   financial participation and single status were found as frequently in unionised as non-unionised firms

    In other words, if this survey is correct, employers moving in the unitary rather than the cooperative direction are more likely to adopt the 'traditional' mode, viewing employees as a commodity, and putting a high priority on cost minimisation.

The RAC

One organisation which consciously moved its stance to the 'sophisticated consultative' mode was the RAC's Rescue Services Division. Management saw worthwhile advantages in establishing a positive relationship with the recognised trade union, the T&GWU, providing this did not impede crucial business decisions. Over a long time, management had gone to considerable lengths to ensure that union officials were well briefed on what was needed to be done to ensure the RAC's continued prosperity, including restraining undue growth in staff and other costs.

When the time came in the early 1990s for the organisation to undergo a really substantial change programme, management was in a good position to open a constructive dialogue with the union. The aim was a challenging one – to achieve organisational change, including job reductions, while retaining and enhancing staff commitment. The union negotiated improved terms for staff affected by closure, and the introduction of a staff support programme. Management gave two vital undertakings:

- to be seen to deliver any promises made during the change period
- fair treatment.

The outcome of the programme was extremely positive. The reaction of personnel director Diana Palmer was that 'a vital ingredient in our success has been the careful management of employee relations with the support and understanding of staff and union representatives'.

Baxi Ltd

The company embarked on a far-reaching process of re-engineering over a number of years.[14] Consistent hard work was needed to win the full support of an initially sceptical workforce. However, through positive information sharing, a position of real trust was established. Processes included formal quarterly meetings with representatives, where all changes were discussed, together with competitor and market analysis. The same information was made available as was available to the board. More responsibility was devolved to the workforce; clocking off was abolished in 1992.

As a result of these efforts, the company reported that pay negotiations were finalised more rapidly and the health and safety record improved. As one example of business benefits, throughput time for manufacturing boilers was reduced from 6 hours to 52 minutes.

The Japanese model of employee relations

Another way of looking at the situation is in terms of the Japanese model, which combines elements of the model set out above and also incorporates particular concepts of its own. The Japanese model is well documented elsewhere, with its special brand of employee involvement and so on. What has always struck me about the Japanese approach is not so much the particular techniques involved, but the thoroughgoing nature of the strategic thinking behind it. To take as an example the issue of single status for staff, if a Japanese company decides that single status is important as part of an overall strategy, then single status is introduced. In so many traditional UK-owned companies, the issue has been debated in a half-hearted kind of way for years, and still not implemented!

Employee relations objectives

There are in effect two strands to any thinking about employee relations (ER). The first is concerned with the formal aspects of the employment relationship, such as collective agreements, procedures, and contractual arrangements. The second embodies what might be called the spirit imbuing these formal arrangements. What are the organisation's underlying employee relations objectives and what values do they reflect?

Under the old agenda, objectives were described in terms of retaining staff, reducing labour turnover and avoiding costly confrontation with the workforce. The new agenda is much more concerned with fostering the commitment of teams and individuals. With flatter structures, with employees dealing direct with clients and taking responsibility for their own quality, the risk to the employer is not the old style withdrawal of labour, but rather the far more subtle withdrawal of discretionary effort.

The concept of discretionary effort

In the modern organisation it is just this discretionary effort that is increasingly vital to provide a competitive edge. Workers may quite adequately complete the daily routine in accordance with their contract and their formal job description but omit that extra element that creates highly satisfied customers. Such action – or rather inaction – is rather like a modern version of the work to rule, always more difficult to deal with than straightforward strike action. By definition, discretionary effort cannot be imposed, certainly not in a sustained way over time.

In effect, we are considering here the new version of an old concept, the psychological contract. The concept that lies at the heart of a healthy contract is trust and such a contract takes full account of the employee agenda. At a recent Institute of Personnel and Development (IPD) National Conference, criticism was voiced of some aspects of Japanese management, which despite the rhetoric can take advantage of individuals. Nissan personnel director Peter Wickens called for an efficient approach to production which respected human values, 'lean, people-centred, volume production', with a 'modus operandi which begins with individuals who then work together to achieve a common goal. We must never achieve higher productivity at the expense of the individuals doing the job'.[15]

Drowned in goodness?

One of the early documents produced by the Personnel Standards Lead Body conveyed the results of interviews with chief executives concerning the personnel function. One respondent criticised an 'indiscriminate approach to being a good employer so that the enterprise was "drowned in goodness"'. While such reservations are understandable, we must guard against them being in reality a cover for a totally hard-nosed 'macho' style of management.

Employers undoubtedly face apparently contradictory pressures; on the one hand, the need to respond to short-term demands to reduce costs and maintain profitability, on the other the need to build and retain employee commitment. The challenge for the personnel function is to help the organisation find the right balance and to manage the tension between these contradictions.

The DVLA

One organisation that has worked hard to find positive answers is the Driver and Vehicle Licensing Agency (DVLA). Around 70 per cent of the DVLA's staff are women and its employee relations policies are consciously 'family friendly'. These include a highly flexible approach to part-time working, job sharing, and a workplace nursery. Management insists that such benefits are not only highly valued by employees, but are also cost effective and make for a highly efficient workforce.[16]

While this organisation's circumstances may be thought unusual, the need for innovative and creative approaches to new ER demands is widespread. This is well illustrated in the LHRG paper *Winning People*, which concludes:

> The loss of long-established trust caused by the culture shift has made it
> hard to manage the inevitable ambiguity caused by a mammoth change
> ... Business re-engineering and staff changes have together improved

productivity and also created a widespread potential for further improvement. The achieved improvement has been through 'working harder'. This has physical limits. The next leap can only come from 'working smarter'. That means tackling cynicism and improving staff motivation.

The employee relations aspects of the new agenda are about the humanities rather than systems and technical procedures. The LHRG report again:

- Changes in staff management systems are important, but even more important is the glue that holds the organisation together.
- Technical manpower planning is important, but even more important are the strategic actions that can make empowerment and employ-ability a reality.

LINKING THEMES

One of the propositions in this book is that the personnel function can no longer afford to be subdivided into discrete disciplines. Just as for organisations as a whole, the function itself needs to be re-engineered. Although I have identified specific topics within the new agenda, the boundaries between these topics are far from clear-cut. There are also three what I have called 'linking themes' which run like a thread through all the topics, and these are:

- the concept of competences
- the international dimension
- the impact of technology

THE CONCEPT OF COMPETENCES

Of all these themes, the notion of competences is the one that has attracted most recent attention. There is now a regular journal devoted exclusively to the subject – in fact, of all the matters covered in this book this is the one in most danger of succumbing to the 'flavour of the month' syndrome.

The concept is based on the identification of 'clusters' of behaviour, underpinned by a set of personal traits, which are deemed to be those of most importance to success in a given job, or indeed across a whole organisation. This of course reflects the move away from an exclusive focus on technical skills to the recognition that these need to be allied to appropriate behaviour. In today's organisations, the excellent technician is relatively ineffective unless he or she is equally able to communicate his or her skills, to contribute them to a team effort, and to influence others.

Once the appropriate competences have been identified, they can be used in the context of recruitment, development and reward; in fact they are relevant to the whole arena of human resource management.

One HR director[17] is quoted as describing the concept of competences in these terms:

- The technique is like glue, allowing firms to align HR initiatives much better, and making it possible to align HR more effectively with business goals in the future.
- It provides a common language for performance and moving forward development.
- It gives line managers a tool to empower them to develop people.
- It contributes to the understanding of what development really means, giving the individual the tools to take responsibility for their own development.

According to a recent survey of competency frameworks[18]:

... competences provide a common cultural thread, a language for success and a framework for thinking about excellence ... a way of communicating about the future, managing open employment relationships and focusing on change.

From Boots to Bass

The concept of competences is relevant to all organisations. Two firms which have been among the leaders in applying the concept in the UK are two very different businesses, Boots the Chemists and brewers Bass.

Boots sees competences as a fundamental part of their approach to performance management. Competence based development 'integrates learning into the workplace, focuses on standards of performance and business results and provides continuous development'.

So far as Bass is concerned, the concept of competences makes personnel strategies business led. The company identified the prime elements of corporate culture which would be crucial to the business in the future:

- developing imaginative versatile people

- encouraging them to support one another across organisational boundaries
- imbuing people of all disciplines with financial literacy
- putting a premium on flexibility, learning and willingness to change
- recognising the pivotal effect of excellent communications.

A whole series of statements was then established, defining the behaviours and characteristics required of employees at all levels if this corporate culture was to be achieved. This competences framework is used to underpin not only development but also reward.

A feature of both these cases was the partnership between personnel and the line in developing such frameworks. For Bass, it was critical to express the competency statements in straightforward language, avoiding 'personnel speak' like the plague. Working parties of line managers were crucial to the process. Boots emphasised a consultative approach, surveying line managers and staff as a whole.

Chase Manhattan

This major financial institution has placed competences at the centre of their approach to every aspect of strategic personnel management, including all the elements of the new agenda discussed earlier. In the mid-'80s, the bank appreciated that their customers were turning into global customers, in large measure as a result of the development of international communications. To respond, a considerable effort was made to determine customer needs, and this led to a definition of corporate core competences.

Internally, the HR function and the line worked together at senior level to identify what people resources the bank had, and to establish a databank of individual competences. This took the bank into the realm of marketing what individuals had to offer against customer needs, a very different concept from the idea of trying to fit people into pre-existing jobs. Staff became empowered to fulfil the demands of customers, rather than of jobs.

This approach incorporates a number of the themes of this book, such as partnership between personnel and the line, and specifically the alliance between personnel and marketing.

Flavour of the month or not, the concept of competences offers a powerful way forward in the search for more strategic clout for the personnel function.

THE INTERNATIONAL DIMENSION

Jan Carlzon of SAS has been quoted as saying that it is 'impossible to run a national policy anymore'. No firm can afford to ignore the international dimension. Previously, a domestic business would perhaps employ an export department, but now all businesses find themselves increasingly enmeshed in an international environment. We saw in a previous chapter the example of the old Tube Investments, with around 60,000 employees almost exclusively in the UK. The modern TI is a totally international business with around 8000 in the UK and 16,000 overseas. Utilities such as British Telecom (BT) and British Gas are clearly looking to international alliances and operations to enable them to prosper in the global economy. One of the issues surrounding the proposed privatisation of the Post Office was how it would be able to fund such international development.

The importance of the international dimension was identified by the IBM/Towers Perrin study. The questionnaire asked respondents to select and rank 5 items from a list of 17 environmental factors affecting human resource management. Two of the factors that emerged as gaining most in importance over the period 1991 to 2000 were the globalisation of business structures and of the economy.

Many organisations, particularly larger ones, are moving away from the old model of separate national operations towards a far more integrated approach. Rosabeth Moss Kantor's dictum that 'what is important is not how responsibilities are divided but how people can pull together to pursue new opportunities' is as true across national boundaries as it is locally. Unilever is one prime example; its national operations have been transformed so that product groups work on a European, even global basis.

The Ashridge Survey

The Ashridge Management Research Group produced important data on the subject in their 1990 survey of global HR strategies.[19] Among the companies surveyed, international HR issues were among the top priorities for the future. The top four reasons for this were given as:

- the Single European Market
- speed of market changes

- mergers and acquisitions
- foreign competition.

The contribution of personnel

In all this there are two challenges for the personnel function. First, the function has to develop international knowledge and expertise, and secondly it has to apply this within the organisation. An important step in this process might well be in the field of culture. National cultures strongly influence management style, values and many other features of a company's operations and in an international firm this has to be understood and managed. Personnel needs to be familiar with the subject if it is to be a player in this arena. The base information available from such studies as those of Trompenaars and Hofstede and a practical grasp of their implications need to be part of the personnel toolkit.[20]

Other parts of the toolkit include competence in the international dimensions of employee relations (the impact of European Union law needs no elaboration), of remuneration and of recruitment.

Equipped with this knowledge and expertise, the function has a crucial role to play in helping the company to be internationally minded. For example, reverting to the topic of cultures, one of the enemies of working together effectively across national boundaries is the often entrenched attitude that our behaviour is the norm, while other nationalities have 'funny' cultures. The fact is of course that our behaviour is equally governed by our own culture, which has its own peculiarities. The first step in understanding and working with others is to understand our own culture and how it influences our business behaviour and reactions. Until this mindset is achieved, cultural differences will continue to be a source of misunderstanding and conflict. If personnel can be a role model in behaving 'internationally' and can work out ways of establishing this as a norm within the organisation, it will already be making a massive contribution towards successful international working.

The particular importance of international management development

The Ashridge survey concluded that management development had emerged as a key issue in establishing a successful international organisation, which puts the ball firmly in personnel's court! The survey listed six key characteristics of the international manager:

- strategic awareness
- adaptability in new situations
- sensitivity to different cultures
- ability to work in international teams
- language skills
- understanding international marketing.

It is perhaps not surprising, but significant nevertheless, that the majority of these characteristics involve 'soft' skills.

Findings from the survey elaborate on this by listing some specific issues:

- planning for international careers – developing managers and the organisation
- ensuring a more positive image for working internationally
- creating a more internationally diverse workforce by recruiting internationally
- preparing managers for international assignments
- developing managers while on assignment to prepare for re-entry
- capturing managers' international learning
- using management education to build the international organisation

The tendency of recent years has been to reduce the number of expatriates because of the costs involved. However, the organisation that is serious about being an international player cannot afford to take this process too far. Apart from the obvious fact that such a policy reduces opportunities for international management development, it leads inevitably to the creation of local 'fiefdoms' and restricts the flow of international information, vital to the firm's progress.

Conclusions

The Survey concludes:

> One of the major tasks is to build a collective learning environment which promotes a sharing of experience and development on a worldwide scale and which fosters an easy dialogue between the different countries and cultures that a company encompasses. The future is not just about international competition or international collaboration: it is also about international learning.

My own conclusion is that the new agenda has developed further since the Ashridge survey. While many major corporations undoubtedly need to be clear about the qualities needed to be a successful global manager, for most organisations this global manager is something of a mythical beast! Of far wider significance is the fact that all managers need to be what I have called 'internationally minded'. This is where the real challenge lies, and the real opportunity for the strategic personnel practitioner.

TECHNOLOGY

The third theme in our model of the new HR agenda is technology. The term 'computerised personnel information systems' (CPISs) is increasingly used, indicating the specialised nature of personnel applications of computer technology. CPISs clearly provide the potential to enhance the strategic contribution in all of the new agenda areas.

Enduring and emerging benefits

The IBM/Towers Perrin study devotes a chapter to the subject. It identifies 7 major CPIS benefits. Of these, two are enduring – ie those that received high importance ratings for 1991 and were also identified as having high potential for improvement by 2000. These are faster information processing and greater accuracy of information. One is reminded of the comment in the Bass case that line management judged the personnel function not only by quality but also speed of response.

The survey also identified what the authors called 'emerging benefits' – ie those that were not seen as currently of top priority but which were identified as having great potential for the year 2000. These were improved planning and programme development and enhanced employee communications. One conclusion from this is that CPISs are currently being used for primarily administrative tasks, but that the potential for more dynamic and strategic benefits is recognised. This ties in with another finding of the survey, that in future the issue of the cost control of the personnel function will be of less significance than the return on investment in human resources.

1994 Computers in Personnel

This conclusion is supported by a quite different study, the 1994 *Computers in Personnel* (CIP) survey.[21] The survey asked participants to rate the extent to which their CPIS helped with some 30 personnel activities. The activities that were stated to help 'to a great extent' were competency information, recruitment, job/skill matching and training administration. However, these were included by less than 20 per cent of participants.

Far more activities were rated as being of help 'to some extent' and these were mentioned by 35 per cent plus. However the activities in this category were the good old chestnuts of employee records, payroll, absence and holiday, and Statutory Sick Pay (SSP) calculations. The survey author concluded:

> There still seems to be a significant difference between personnel claiming as a profession that we need to re-engineer our jobs and automate our administrative processes and the added value our CPISs are providing. As a developing profession, human resources has so much further to go and after analysing the 1994 CIP survey I am left with the feeling that we are still using only a very small proportion of the benefits IT [information technology] has to offer us.

Technology and the line

A particular aspect of this issue is the involvement of line management. Of the 1994 CIP survey respondents 75 per cent agreed that 'managers don't know what information is available'. The IBM/Towers Perrin study concurs, finding that currently less than 20 per cent of executives and supervisors have any significant access to the CPIS in their organisation. But for the year 2000, a substantial change is anticipated. In the future, nearly 60 per cent will have a great deal of access.

This is in tune with the concept of the personnel/line partnership, which I have identified at many points in this book as a critical part of the strategic approach.

Conclusions

1. Information technology will be of increasing importance to any attempt to manage the personnel function in a strategic way.
2. This means applying it creatively to all the items on the new agenda.
3. Executives and line management will need more access to CIPSs, in conjunction with personnel.

Key questions
● In terms of current practice, what are the key functional areas in your own operation?
● Are you satisfied that these reflect the right strategic priorities?
● In the case of each area, at what level of involvement are you operating?
● Are you satisfied with the level of competence you are able to deploy in these areas?

Notes

1. *Personnel Management*, July 1994, p20.
2. Tyson, Shaun and Witcher, Michael (1994) 'Getting in Gear: Post-Recession HR Management' *Personnel Management* August pp20–3.
3. Kessler, Ian and Purcell, John (1990–3) *The Performance Related Pay Research Project* Oxford Institute for Employee Relations.
4. Thompson, Marc *Pay and Performance: the employees' experience*, see Bibliography.
5. Murlis, Helen (1994) 'The challenge of rewarding teamwork' *Personnel Management* February p8.
6. Pickard, Jane (1993) 'How Incentives can Drive Teamworking' *Personnel Management* September pp26–7, 29, 31–2.
7. An Oxford Training case study.
8. *Building the Empowered Organisation* Kinsley Lord monograph.
9. *Personnel Management* (1994) February p48.
10. An Oxford Training case study.
11. *Personnel Management* (1993) December p17.
12. Purcell, John and Ahlstrand, Bruce (1994) *Human Resource Management in the Multi-Divisional Company* Oxford University Press, Oxford.
13. Millward, Neil, Stevens, Mark, Smart, David and Hawes, W R (1992) *Workplace Industrial Relations in Transition*, see Bibliography.
14. Baxi Partnership, a case study from Harvey, David *Re-engineering: the critical success factors*, see Bibliography.
15. *Personnel Management* (1993) 'All is not perfect with Japanese management' February p12.
16. *Personnel Management Plus* (1994) 'Why it pays to be family-friendly' February p20.
17. Refausse John, Director of HR Development at Hiram Walker (1994) *Personnel Management* July, p38.
18. Wisher, Vicky (1994) 'Competencies: the precious seeds of growth', *Personnel Management*, July.

19. Barham, Kevin and Wills, Stefan *Management across Frontiers – identifying the competences of successful international managers*, see Bibliography.
20. Trompenaars, F *Riding the Waves of Culture*, see Bibliography.
21. *Personnel Management* (1994) *Computers in Personnel* survey, July p55.

8

Leadership – The Role of the HR Director

"Ownership of people issues and understanding of people
management at top management level is essential.
Without leadership from the top and the promotion of people
management strategies from this level, progress elsewhere in the
organisation will be difficult to initiate and impossible to sustain".
Managing People – the Changing Frontiers, IPD paper

This book is about helping personnel practitioners at all levels to take a more strategic view of their role. Most readers will not be working at board level – at least not yet ! Yet it is clearly pertinent for us to look at the issues surrounding the leadership of the function within organisations. Should there be a personnel representative on boards of companies? If so, what are the most important aspects of the role, and what are the necessary qualifications for the job, particularly in the future?

I argue that people are increasingly the key to competitive edge and at the heart of issues critical to survival and success in the years ahead. From this, one has to conclude that the function with direct responsibility and expertise in the people area must be represented within the top team of the organisation.

POTENTIAL IMPACT OF THE HR DIRECTOR

A 1993 survey by Warwick and Sheffield Universities of 176 firms in the UK suggested that those companies with a personnel director on the board are more effectively managed.[1] The survey showed conclusively that personnel is much more likely to have an influence on strategic issues when there is a personnel director on the main board. Some of the issues picked out by the study were:

- the career development of senior managers
- the design of senior management incentive schemes and performance related pay
- setting and reviewing performance targets
- linking HR strategies to the board's agenda

Did the involvement of personnel at board level improve the organisation's handling of these issues? Alas, the survey was not equipped to provide direct evidence. However, it seems reasonable to assume that such matters are likely to be better handled where there is competent and experienced personnel input at the policy-making stage.

Board responsibilities

A study conducted by the Institute of Directors (IOD) and Henley Management College set out four primary tasks considered to be essential board responsibilities.[2] These were:

- establishing a company's vision, mission and values
- setting strategy and structure
- supervising management
- exercising responsibility to shareholders.

Whilst none of these is the exclusive preserve of the personnel function, a number of them cry out for a sound personnel contribution.

Survey evidence

What is the current position? The IBM/TPFC *21st Century Vision* agrees that the positioning of the senior personnel executive is a crucial issue:

> Having a head of HR report directly to the CEO or another top line executive certainly supports the goal of linking HR more closely to business strategy and objectives. There was nearly universal agreement among our respondents that heads of HR should report to a CEO or line executive. This indicates a view that if HR–line partnerships are to work, they must start at the top of the organisation.

This was borne out in practice – 74 per cent of respondents indicated that this was the situation within their organisation.

This seems to be a very positive finding, but we have to treat it with caution. For one thing, only a minority of respondents were from the UK, and also the finding does not necessarily mean actual membership of the board. A contrast is provided by the Warwick/Sheffield study which found that less than 50 per cent had a personnel director on the board. Moreover it was foreign-owned companies which were more likely to have such a director (54 per cent of such firms), compared to UK domestic companies (22 per cent). UK multinational companies showed some increase at 24 per cent.

Why so few HR directors?

In one sense, this goes a long way to explain why the personnel function often seems to lack real clout, and why many personnel professionals settle for an operational or even administrative role. Yet it is only a symptom; the deeper question is, why do only a minority of firms have personnel directors on their boards?

One might suggest three possible reasons.

The first is that the leadership team of the organisation may not fully recognise the strategic nature of the human resource. This requires no further comment, except to say that such a team still has a lot to learn!

A second reason could be that the team believes it has the necessary competence in the HR area without the need for a specialist director. This kind of thinking tends to come from the 'common sense' school of human resource management; in other words, managing people is a matter of common sense and requires no particular expertise.

Thirdly, top management may assume that such a director would come from the ranks of the personnel professionals within the organisation – and that none of these professionals is regarded as board material. We certainly have to admit that the professional development of personnel people often fails to equip them for a board role.

Personnel on the board

There is much confusion surrounding this whole issue of a Personnel presence on the board. We would certainly not wish to argue that the senior personnel professional in the organisation should be on the board, as it were ex officio. What is more, in smaller companies it may well be right for a board member to have more than one portfolio of responsibility, including personnel.

The CEO as personnel director?

It is sometimes argued that people are so important that the Chief Executive is in effect his or her own personnel director. I do not buy that argument. Of course it is to be hoped that the CEO will provide first class leadership and will have a good 'feel' for people. But the fact remains that he or she has to take a balanced view of all the firm's resources and its responsibilities to its various stakeholders. One hopes that the CEO has a sound grasp of finance, but that does not enable him or her to dispense with a finance director. No, we must be unequivocal; an appropriate member of the board other than the CEO should be clearly designated as having the board responsibility for HR.

Personnel v HR ... again

This is where we need to return to the issue of personnel v HR. Early in the book, I suggested that we could usefully draw the distinction between the *personnel function* – the group of personnel professionals offering necessary and important specialist expertise – and *human resource management* – all those aspects of managing people for which the line has to take equal responsibility. I drew the parallel with finance. All managers have a financial responsibility, but they do not have to be accountants. Similarly, the board member concerned is named the finance director. The chief accountant on the other hand does not normally hold a board position.

Thus for the human resource. The relevant board member has to take an overview of all people issues – this is different from heading up the personnel function. It will normally incorporate that role but it involves other strategic duties and oversight. For that reason, the chapter heading refers to the HR director.

It follows that the appropriate person may not necessarily be a personnel professional in the strict sense. On the other hand, it is no solution to give the portfolio to a board member who does not have the knowledge or experience to handle it in a competent and effective manner. In other words, the 'common sense' school won't wash!

I deal later with the attributes and skills required of the HR director, but first we need to look more deeply at the job description.

The HR director's key purpose

A statement of the *key purpose* of the role might look something like this:

To ensure that people issues are taken fully into account in all the board's considerations, and specifically that they are given full weight in the determination of the company's strategic objectives; and to provide leadership in all aspects of human resource management.

There is no doubt that such a role is a demanding one. Moreover, if taken seriously, it has substantial implications for the way the company is run. To give three examples. It brings the HR director into the heart of the debate about the relative importance of different stakeholders and the rewards due to them of successful enterprise. Employees are seen not as a cost of production but as a key investment. What is their appropriate share of the value added, as compared to other claims, such as shareholder dividends and the remuneration of board members?

Another example would be the people implications of a merger or acquisition. As noted elsewhere, one of the principal reasons why so many mergers fail is that they are seen in purely financial or market terms, with little or no regard to the human resource aspects. The HR director will insist that the people ramifications are taken seriously as part of the decision-making process. This implies that the human resources, competences and policies of the organisation to be acquired should be as carefully studied as other aspects.

Downsizing is another highly sensitive area where one would look to the HR director to play a decisive role. No board should embark lightly on a process where employees are deprived of their livelihood. This is not to imply that such action is not sometimes necessary for the health of the business, but the HR director must ensure that redundancy is viewed as a last resort, and is handled with skill and sensitivity.

Unless there is someone on the board with clear accountability for these and other critical HR matters, it is unlikely that the people aspects of strategic decisions will be given their due weight. Moreover, the strategic partnership which I have emphasised earlier between personnel and other functions needs to begin at board level. It is the HR director who needs to provide the leadership and foresight to develop and sustain this partnership.

RESPONSIBILITIES OF THE HR DIRECTOR

Having stated the key purpose, the job description for the HR director will set out specific responsibilities and these may embrace many of the standard personnel functions that we have already discussed, dependent on the particular type of organisation and its priorities. However, I would like to focus on a number of areas which might not feature so commonly in the job description. These are:

- to propagate the vision of the future within the organisation
- to reflect to top management what is happening in the organisation
- to stimulate the HR aspects of the business plan
- to spearhead the alliance with the marketing function
- to be the guardian of ethical standards within the business.

To propagate the vision of the future within the organisation

To give of their best people need to be able to make sense of the organisation they work for. They need to feel that it is 'all of a piece'. This means that the way it is organised, the decisions that are made, the way senior management behave, should hang together in a coherent fashion. According to the IPD position paper, 'in too many organisations inconsistency between what is said and what is done undermines trust, generates employee cynicism and provides evidence of contradictions in management thinking'. Above all, employees need to feel that the organisation has a future and that they are part of that future.

An important part of the HR director's leadership role is to propagate this sense of coherence within the organisation. This means being able to monitor what is happening within the organisation and maintaining a sense of how the generality of employees are feeling. This involves walking the job, and also taking opportunities to meet groups of staff, perhaps on training courses, or on semi-social kinds of occasions. These events enable two way communication, providing feedback as to how staff see things, and giving the director a chance to explain, for example, the reasons underlying a certain decision or policy.

The director will also need to rely on feedback provided by personnel staff. Formal employee surveys have their place too in this communications process.

Being informed is one thing; taking action is another. The HR director has to have sufficient influence to ensure that employees' views and perspectives are taken into account. Where a particular policy is not coherent with the kind of organisation the company is trying to build, it will need to be modified. To quote the PSLB's *A Perspective on Personnel*: the HR director must 'exercise judgment in supporting or opposing executive actions – providing a balancing and opposing force, when the actions may be cost effective in the short term but damaging to morale and productivity at the time or in the longer term'.

As to a vision of the future, this can only be propagated if there is such a vision shared at the top level. The HR director should be involved in bringing this about. This may well be a substantial challenge, particularly as vision building does not come naturally to everybody and some board colleagues will be happier dealing with the realm of immediate facts.

To reflect to top management what is happening in the organisation

Board members can reasonably look to their HR colleague to keep them informed on the state of 'public opinion' within the organisation. How is employee morale? What has been the reaction to a particular policy decision? If we make a certain change, will it prove acceptable to the staff involved? The HR director will need to be skilled in estimating potential reactions, and avoiding nasty surprises. His or her reputation will suffer if a particular decision leads to unhappy consequences, such as key staff leaving or industrial action, where he or she has not at least forewarned his or her colleagues of the potential risks before the decision was taken.

C K Prahalad shed some fascinating light on this process in a speech to the 1994 IPD national conference:[3]

> We need to understand the 'cognitive maps' of people inside the organisation, the processes by which those maps evolve, and the processes of collective learning and socialisation. Then how to *forget this past* becomes a more important prerequisite to learning about the future. Our problem is not learning new things per se; rather, it is letting go of what we know. It is managing the forgetting curve.

Prahalad also points out that:

> ... we spend an enormous amount of time talking about competitive strategies, expectations of people, measures of performance and behaviour, and so on, but very little asking, what is the quality of the lens? the quality of interpretation of the evolving dynamics of industries.

It is not too fanciful to see the HR director as this lens, at least in so far as relationships within the firm are concerned.

In this context, the HR director may well forge a particular relationship with the CEO. As the Personnel Standards Lead Body document put it, the HR director must 'read the organisation' for the chief executive. The CEO especially will wish to feel well informed as to what is happening in the organisation, and should feel confident in relying on his or her HR director to provide an accurate perspective. This will sometimes mean the HR director giving unwelcome advice – on those occasions, one has to hope it will not be a case of 'shoot the messenger'!

To stimulate the HR aspects of the business plan

One of the themes of this book has been the need to view human resources from a strategic perspective, as part of overall business objectives. This can only be done effectively at board level, and must be one of the most important tasks of the HR director.

Again, Prahalad has some important observations to make:

> Growth must have some relationship to the skill base of the organisation … Today it is widely recognised that competition is taking place at three levels. It takes place in end products, and in price battles; but it is also taking place at the level of core competencies, as companies try to build the capacity to lead the evolution of new industries and the development of new products and gateways to the future. A core competence is carried in the heads of individuals and teams. Of course there is a technical component, but more crucial is the social organisation, the capacity of people to share information and to continuously redeploy knowledge. To me that may be the more fundamental battle taking place between large companies.

Purcell sees human resources at the second level of strategic thinking, as it were halfway between fundamental strategic objectives and their implementation in operational terms. In Prahalad's terms, however, it is the company's capacity to 'leverage resources' that creates strategic opportunities. This brings the HR director into the heart of the business planning process.

To spearhead the alliance with the marketing function

I have already dealt in some detail with this issue of strategic alliances with other functions. It is a concept that is viable at different levels of the organisation; it may be just as important to a relatively junior personnel officer as it is at board level. Nevertheless, in strategic terms it is particularly crucial between board members representing the different functions.

As it happened, at the time of writing, the link between human resource management and marketing, at least in terms of public relations, was illustrated in a particularly graphic way over a controversy regarding senior executive remuneration. A substantial increase in the reward package of the chief executive of a high profile organisation came into the public domain at the same time as the announcement of staff cutbacks. The result was a disaster in public relations and political terms. Whether fairly or not, the impression was given that internal HR and external affairs were regarded as entirely separate matters, managed in watertight compartments.

To be the guardian of ethical standards within the business

This again is a topic I have already dealt with in some detail. It might be asked why this responsibility should fall particularly to the HR director. Indeed, the IBM/TPFC study on a vision of HR for the 21st century does not mention it in any direct way and it is true to say that it has ramifications for virtually all aspects of business.

On the other hand, if it does not specifically feature among the responsibilities of a particular director portfolio, it is just the kind of issue that will fall between every stool.

I would argue that it is essentially a people issue and that personnel people are best suited to handle it by experience and even perhaps by inclination. So, in my book, it falls to the HR director – another challenge!

Beyond the job description

In rereading these reflections on key purpose and responsibilities, I wonder if the words have captured the real essence of the HR director's role. Let us turn to Prahalad again:

> Unfortunately we have created an approach to business management where the human dimensions of creativity, curiosity, and a need for belonging to a community have been taken out. There is too much debate about management, too little debate about the totality of the human being. *Competing for the Future* says that if we can shape an aspiration which by design is beyond the resources of the company and share the excitement of striving for it, then we can create entrepreneurial drive instead of a large bureaucracy.
>
> It is important to re-create the capacity to dream in a large organisation. Ask the question: is it worth doing? A significant role of top

management is about creating and deploying resources, not just allocating them.

ATTRIBUTES REQUIRED OF THE HR DIRECTOR

So, if you are aspiring to a board level position, what skills and attributes should you have – or seek to develop? The Personnel Standards Lead Body conducted a series of interviews with chief executives to determine the essential requirements for effectiveness.[4] This elicited some forthright criticism, and a list of 'don'ts'. Too many personnel professionals, it seems, 'emphasise specialist skills to the detriment of both business understanding and the ability to act as an accepted consultant'. They show:

- an over-conscious concern with rules and procedures amounting sometimes to inappropriate policing and blocking action
- a tendency to introduce systems and procedures which failed because they did not fit the business and/or were not owned by management
- an indiscriminate approach to being a 'good employer'.

A director first

The right approach for any executive director is to see themselves as a director first, and a functional specialist second. I referred earlier in this chapter to the draft standards published by the IOD in conjunction with Henley Management College. Following in-depth responses from 340 experienced directors, they have identified essential qualities for an executive director, and these are just as relevant to the HR director as to any other executive member of the board (see Table 8.1).

Evidence from consultants MCP

As part of the preparation for this book, colleagues from consultants MCP and I set up a survey of some 26 senior personnel professionals, all of them at or around board level.[5] They were asked to rate nine factors in terms of establishing their own credibility, influence and standing within their organisation. The highest rated factors in order of importance were:

- knowledge of the business
- personal relationship with the boss and with colleagues
- quality of service provided.

Table 8.1   *The personal qualities and areas of knowledge needed in the boardroom*

The six groups of personal qualities are:
1.   Strategic perception and decision-making
2.   Analytical understanding
3.   Communication
4.   Interacting with others
5.   Board management
6.   Achieving results

The areas of knowledge are in three groups:
1.   Specific to boards
2.   Specific to the company
3.   Relating to the business environment

Source: Institute of Directors 1995

Of lower importance were:

- knowledge of employment legislation
- personnel expertise
- general professional knowledge and understanding.

On the other hand, when asked which of these factors was *the* most important for a personnel director, the response was somewhat different:

- for 44 per cent it was knowledge of the business
- for 20 per cent it was professional knowledge and understanding
- for 20 per cent it was input into strategic thinking.

This implies that personal skills and relationships are key to establishing credibility and influence, but these 'soft' skills must be underpinned by a sound framework of professional expertise. What is certainly clear was that knowledge of the business was regarded by these respondents as a *sine qua non*.

A European perspective

The IMD report prepared in 1992 for the European Association for Personnel Management, *The Emerging Role of the HR Manager in Europe*, looked at this issue from two perspectives. First, it included the question, 'What kind of knowledge and skills do you think will be important to you in the mid-1990s?'. Secondly, it considered criteria used to select senior personnel executives.

The first question asked respondents to rate nine areas of knowledge and skill. The most highly rated proved to be:

- organisational change and change management
- individual values and motivation concepts
- knowledge of working in teams, and consultation skills.

The findings concerning selection criteria present a different picture. Major points included:

- the top human resource job is becoming much more business oriented
- the dominant consideration in selecting the head of HR is 'fit' with the CEO
- the head of human resources requires management capability and leadership qualities
- character and certain personality attributes are more important than specific skills
- succession to the top HR job is no longer automatically from the function.

The conclusions of the report support those of our MCP survey:

> to be considered the equals of line managers, to hold equivalent status, to receive comparable rewards, personnel/HR managers may henceforth have to think and act in business, rather than functional terms. From this point of view, functional experience and expertise are necessary but insufficient criteria for success. They do not ensure ultimate business effectiveness. As one CEO remarked, 'we don't make financial, marketing or human resource decisions – we make business decisions ... This requires personnel/HR managers who not only deliver impeccable PM [personal management]/HR services and manage well the development of people, but who are also knowledgeable about the firm's central competencies, key values, competitive environment and customer demands'.

A summary

A brief summary of the attributes needed by the HR director might be:

- *Professional*
  — broad knowledge of business and ability to relate this to your own organisation

— ability to manage change processes
— capacity to deliver world-class personnel services
— a belief in developing the capability of people in the organisation
● *Personal*
   — confidence and self-respect
   — excellent influencing, negotiating and consulting skills, being able to press your case
   — ability to develop empathy with board colleagues and CEO
   — cross-cultural sensitivity.

HANDLING THE ROLE ON THE BOARD

What leads to success in a board role? While it is important to have the right mixture of skills and experience, this is by no means the whole story. We cannot ignore the realities of power and politics, an inevitable ingredient in any organisation, especially among those able and ambitious enough to have reached board level. This means that success is very closely allied to survival. In most commercial situations, people want to do a good job – but they also want to survive (unless of course they are negotiating for a golden farewell!)

Looked at from this kind of perspective, there are two ways of success: doing a competent job, and persuading others that you are doing a competent job. Unfortunately, in the hard school of life the first by no means automatically leads to the second. What's more, is it too cynical to say that the second does not necessarily even include the first? And that for survival the second is the more important? Although most of us aim to achieve both, we ignore these realities of organisational life at our peril.

Plan to survive

It is also true that survival at the top level depends to some extent on luck, on the way the cards fall in various situations. Not for nothing have we coined the phrase 'more by luck than judgment'. Nevertheless, the HR director cannot afford merely to sit back in a political environment and hope for the best. We need to make our own luck by formulating a strategy for survival.

Some elements of such a strategy are as follows:

- *Being able to sense dangerous issues and acting effectively to defuse them*
  Seemingly innocuous matters have a habit of turning septic and
  causing political damage. The effective director will spot these at a
  distance and head them off.

- *Understanding the levers of power in an organisation and being able to
  handle them judiciously* Some people find it much easier to get things
  done in an organisation than others. This is not just a question of
  seniority, but more about knowing how to exercise power.

- *Cultivating allies and avoiding enemies* In the natural course of things,
  chemistry works well between certain individuals and less well with
  others. We cannot expect to get on equally sympathetically with
  everybody. In the question of allies, it is important to distinguish
  between those who are on the same wavelength in only a superficial
  way, and those whose support will be wholehearted when the chips
  are down. In the case of more difficult relationships, the temptation is
  to avoid the individual concerned, but in fact it is vital to take every
  appropriate business opportunity to keep the line of communication
  open. Where one has a disagreement with a colleague, the golden
  rule is to tackle it face to face.

- *Judging when to press ahead and when to back off* The HR director must
  be able to stand his or her ground and fight his or her corner.
  Becoming susceptible to bullying tactics is usually fatal to survival in
  the end. On the other hand not every battle involves genuine matters
  of principle, and knowing when and how to show flexibility is an
  important art.

- *Knowing when to pass on information* The well-regarded HR director
  will be used as a sounding board on a whole range of topics, even on
  matters outside the HR arena. These will often reflect on personal
  relationships and it is vital to retain the trust of colleagues and
  maintain confidentiality. On the other hand, it will sometimes be
  necessary to pass on information, notably to the CEO. In fact, on
  some occasions the information will be given with the unspoken
  intention that it *will* be passed on. In other words, the HR director is
  used as an impartial conduit. Needless to say, these situations
  demand considerable diplomatic judgment. The HR director who is
  invariably able to get it right will exercise great influence and power;
  if he or she gets it wrong, he or she is dead in the water!

- *Maintaining integrity* Nothing in this part of the book should be seen
  as an encouragement to 'play politics'. Those who live by the sword –
  etc.

A spectrum of team roles

As a member of the board team, the HR director in particular is called upon to play a variety of roles, and it is important to recognise which hat you are wearing at any given moment. The spectrum of power and influence shown in Figure 8.1 illustrates this. On the left-hand side, the director is exercising authority, either in a formal decision-making role as 'executive' or an informal one as 'power broker'. On the right-hand side, the role is more concerned with influence. At the extreme, 'listener', the director is not even called upon to respond; in the 'sounding board' role, it is appropriate to give a reaction, although to a lesser degree than 'coaching' or 'counselling'. The 'clarifier' is called on to put across to colleagues a particular decision or policy, without necessarily being seen as the 'advocate'.

The point along the spectrum which it is appropriate to adopt depends on a variety of circumstances, including:

- the power relationships involved
- the expectations of 'clients' (ie CEO and board colleagues)
- the extent to which the issue concerned is a direct HR responsibility.

The effective HR director will maintain excellent relationships with his or her colleagues, even with those where the chemistry is not a natural fit. The characteristics of such quality relationships are:

executive
      power broker
            advocate
                  clarifier
                        coach or counsellor
                                  sounding board
                                        listener

proactive..*reactive*

power..*influence*

executive...*advisory*

Figure 8.1   *The spectrum of power and influence*

- credibility, stemming from –
  - — professional knowledge
  - — skills
  - — personal qualities
  - — perceived contribution
  - — power base
- trust
- confidentiality
- proper use of power/influence
- shared values and integrity.

THE HR DIRECTOR AS LEADER OF THE PERSONNEL FUNCTION

I started this chapter with a quotation concerning leadership. The HR director is called on to exercise leadership both within the board, and as leader of his or her own professional function. As far as the latter goes, some considerations are as follows:

- The personnel department should be regarded as a model for the rest of the organisation, when it comes to the quality of people management. It is very much a question of 'practise what you preach' or 'do as I say *and* as I do'. Unfortunately, some personnel departments are notoriously badly managed, which does little for the credibility of their work. So, all the issues we have discussed about the style of management in today's world come sharply into focus. *The HR director should be the best coach in the business.*
- This brings into play the development of personnel staff. The department should provide a practical example of a learning organisation. Professional qualifications will doubtless be encouraged, but what of personal skills? what of the skills of consultancy, negotiating and counselling? what of the skills of 'pressing your case'?
- The staff need to be helped to develop business skills; the most junior personnel officer should be able to develop a spreadsheet and read a balance sheet.
- Personnel staff need encouragement to develop their careers. This should increasingly mean gaining line management experience – and that will involve allowing some of your best people to move on.
- What degree of centralisation is appropriate? what should be the role of the centre, and what resources does it need?

Finally, for the HR director to be an effective leader demands two other essentials. These are to do with support both up and down:

- If difficult decisions have been made by the board, it is vital to support those decisions, even if you don't agree with them, and even if they affect your staff adversely.
- In return, when the chips are down, it is equally vital to be seen to support your staff,

SOME CONCLUSIONS

1. For any organisation which recognises the key role of people in securing competitive advantage, it is important to have a competent director on the Board with specific HR responsibility.
2. This does not imply that the senior personnel professional should be on the Board ex officio – but nor is it an appropriate solution to appoint an executive with no personnel experience.
3. We may advance a number of reasons why only a minority of boards of British companies include an HR director, but it is reasonable to question whether present approaches to the development of personnel practitioners equip them adequately for the task.
4. Critical to success in the board role is business understanding. This can be gained in a variety of ways, but ideally involves previous line management experience.

Key questions for the HR director

- How do you measure your particular role? When performing the role excellently, what is happening? If you were absent for an extended period, what would suffer in the business?

- How would you describe the expectations of your clients?

- What are your values in the job? What is important to you? What kind of issues are critical?

- What are the current opportunities to improve your contribution? What are the forces impeding a larger contribution? what are those encouraging it?

- Is uncertainty/confusion an important element in the current situation in the business? What could you do to reduce uncertainty within the board and elsewhere in the organisation?

Notes

1. Marginson, P, Armstrong, P, Edwards P and Purcell, J with Hubbard, N (1993) *The control of industrial relations in large companies: initial analysis of the 1992 company-level industrial relations survey* Warwick Papers in Industrial Relations no 45 December.
2. Institute of Directors (1995) *Good Practice for Directors – Standards for the Board*.
3. Prahalad, C K (1995) 'How HR can help to win the future' *People Management* 12 January pp34–6.
4. Personnel Standards Lead Body (1993) *A Perspective on Personnel* p24.
5. Dearlove, Desmond (1993) 'A key to the boardroom door' *The Times*, December, p16.

Part Four

Strategy is Reading the Future

It is a truism that things will not be the same tomorrow as they are today. A characteristic of the strategic approach is that it takes account of likely future developments. We know that we have no crystal ball and that not all of our prognostications will turn out to be correct. Nevertheless this is no reason to be fatalistic and to rely simply on responding to what comes up. That way we are bound to get some nasty surprises, and if there is one thing senior managers want to avoid it is something unforeseen and nasty coming out of the woodshed.

Personnel people worth their salt will look ahead and undertake some contingency planning. What's more, personnel professionals are in a good position to influence aspects of future developments in the HR field. As a partner of line management, you may justifiably be expected to forewarn of new developments, to interpret them and to help manage them as they begin to impact in real ways.

Chapter 9 suggests some of the factors that are relevant to the work of personnel, under three headings. The first concerns issues of a domestic nature, such as the influence of demographic and social change. The second tackles the potential impact of regulation. Regulation comes in different forms and from different directions and is an increasingly unavoidable factor in organisational life.

Thirdly, we return to less tangible issues under the heading 'The vision thing'. This is an appropriate note on which to close the book. All strategy depends on having some kind of vision of the future. The exciting thing is that we can all own a small part of the big picture and develop it for ourselves.

9

The Need to Look Ahead

"Changes on a global scale are already upon us, as the era known as industrial society gives place to something new. In almost every sphere of life and in a brief span of time the future is being shaped by action or by default. The very assumptions of our culture are now open to debate in new ways".

Faith in the City, *report of the Archbishop of Canterbury's Commission on Urban Priority Areas*

If personnel is a learning system, one of the things it has to learn about is reading the future. If we accept that change is constant, we must accept that the environment in which we are operating will be substantially different in ten, or even five years' time, from what it is today, both within the organisation and externally. Thinking in decades, we worked in a vastly different climate in the '80s, as compared with the '70s, and things are different again in the '90s. With change accelerating, what will we be coping with by the turn of the century and beyond?

If thinking and acting strategically means anything, it involves taking a view beyond today's immediate demands, and proactively creating our own future. Clearly we are limited by developments outside our immediate control, but at least if we anticipate these and think ahead accordingly we can be better masters of our own destiny, rather than being simply buffeted by the winds of 'outrageous fortune'.

This is true of persons, of our function, and of organisations generally. Lloyd's of London is a glaring example of an organisation which failed to do this, and has been struggling to catch up with events ever since. Its survival depends on its ability once again to get ahead of the game. Incidentally, it has not perhaps been sufficiently recognised that the Lloyd's disaster was as much a failure of human resource management as of anything else. One senses that the same scenario could face the whole of the City, and Rajan's comments in *Winning People* point to the HR aspects of this. At the time of writing, events at two of the UK's most prestigious financial institutions, Warburg's and Baring's, are sounding the alarm.

Riding 'white waters'

Organisations must navigate the 'white waters' of social, political and economic change. The personnel function is well placed to play a positive role in this navigation; in fact it could be said that it has a duty to do so, bearing in mind that such change fundamentally affects both the way organisations work and the relationships within them. The role includes:

- *Spotting and monitoring relevant trends*, and advising on their potential implications. Personnel can offer an important window to the outside world, helping to ensure that the organisation does not become too insular.
- *Helping managers to understand the changing environment* and to operate appropriately within it. This can be in general policy terms, perhaps requiring formal training, or it may be more a question of advising and coaching individuals.
- In particular, *advising on new or potential employment legislation*, including the development of case law.
- *Representing the organisation, and bringing its influence to bear*, notably at professional institute, or trade association, level. Personnel professionals have the chance to contribute personally; recent examples have been the Personnel Standards Lead Body, and the RSA Inquiry, let alone of course to their own Institute.

The future – an overview

The rest of this chapter takes a brief overview of some current trends which may well be crucial for the future. The agenda of a recent conference organised by the campaigning organisation Charter 88 gives some idea of the scope of these trends. Topics included:

- Public values, consumer needs – identifying the gap
- Organisational citizenship
- Openness and the right to know
- Scrutiny
- Shareholder and consumer rights.

This looks a pretty indigestible menu! In an attempt to make some sense of it, let's use three categories: domestic, regulatory, and visionary.

DOMESTIC

There are many signs that current patterns of work may be in for a radical overhaul. There is now general acceptance that the concept of a job for life has passed and organisations are beginning to implement some new approaches. For the time being, such changes are mostly tentative and the majority of work is still based on the industrial pattern of 'nine to five'. Nevertheless, it seems likely that this will change in the post-industrial society.

American consultant, William Bridges, believes that the social and cultural infrastructure for the new kind of work is lagging behind the technical.[1] He goes as far as stating that the concept of a 'job' has outlived its usefulness. His answer to the question 'what do people do without jobs?' is 'working within organisations under arrangements that are too fluid and idiosyncratic to be called jobs'.

What are some of the factors creating this situation?

The problem of overload

One senior industrialist got into hot water when he justified his salary in terms of the number of hours he put into the job, 70 hours a week. When challenged on the basis that junior doctors worked just as hard, he commented that he would gladly swap their schedule for his. Some senior managers clearly thrive on what a newspaper article described as 'the long working days, the papers to read at night, the business dinners and the permanent jetlag'. But if we are honest, this is not a lifestyle that appeals to many.

Unfortunately, the demand to endure such workloads is not confined to the top. It seems clear that while increasing numbers are facing enforced idleness, those in work are under pressure to work ever harder. In some cases, such pressure may be in one sense 'legitimate' – the struggle to survive in a harshly competitive world, with ever fewer people employed to do the work. In others, it may have more to do with a 'macho' culture, where you only get on, or even survive, if you are regularly seen to burn, if not the midnight, at least the seven o'clock oil.

Is the price worth paying?

Whatever the motive, there is a price to be paid. As one newspaper headline put it 'Families and profit in peril as firms push staff too hard'. Such a situation must be detrimental to married and family life, with subsequent ill-effects on children. The 1994 project on Corporate Performance conducted by the Institute of Work Psychology at the University of Sheffield found conclusive evidence that higher ratings for production pressure were related to poorer mental health. It would be surprising if the same could not be said of physical well-being and indeed, Cary Cooper, Professor of Organisational Psychological at UMIST, claims that alcoholism, coronary artery disease and a wide range of other stress-related illnesses in the workplace are costing British industry billions of pounds.

In Cary and Rachel Cooper's book, *Living with Stress*, they categorise six sources of work stress:

- *Intrinsic to the job* This includes poor working conditions, lack of safety management, work overload or underload, and mismatch between individual and job.
- *Role in the organisation* Many employees suffer from role ambiguity and conflicts stemming from a lack of clarity of organisational boundaries.
- *Career development* This has been found to be a fundamental stressor at work, in terms of the impact of over-promotion, lack of job security, and thwarted ambition.
- *Relationships at work* This heading includes not only poor relationships with subordinates and colleagues, but also conflict between the employee's own values and those of the organisation.
- *Organisation climate* This includes such factors as a lack of participation in the decision-making process and restrictions on behaviour.
- *Home/work interface* Work stresses can produce tensions within the home environment that only exacerbate the situation.

The Health and Safety Executive has estimated that more than 40 million working days a year are lost in Britain because of stress-related illness.

There is much anecdotal evidence that fear is a powerful reality in many workplaces. Employees are fearful of admitting any problems or weakness lest they should be next 'for the chop'. Older staff admit to counting the years to retirement – somewhat reminiscent (for those of us who can remember!) of the eternal cry of the National Serviceman 'only 435 days to push!' On the face of it, such attitudes do not bode well for the continuing health of the organisation, let alone of its staff.

What do people want?

The hectic materialism and individualism of the '80s has given way to more reflective attitudes, with an appreciation by many that we cannot go on like this. Something has to give. Drucker touched on this tension, when he described the new social challenge: 'The economic challenge will be the productivity of knowledge work and the knowledge worker. The social challenge will however be the dignity of the second class in post capitalist society: the service workers'.

The female influence

One countervailing force is the vastly increased presence of women in the workforce. Of those joining the labour force in the UK between 1987 and 1995, no less than 83 per cent were women. Fifty per cent of women of working age were engaged in the labour force in 1973; by 1991 this had risen to 60 per cent +. Women are less likely to succumb to the maladies of the workaholic. Not only do they have less inclination to work all hours, there are powerful domestic forces which make it extremely difficult for them to do so in many cases.

It is a fair argument that women are placed at a disadvantage as a result of these circumstances. On the other hand, this may prove to be beneficial to society as a whole if it leads to employers' having to review management practice in social areas.

A view from the CBI

At a conference in April 1994, Howard Davies, director-general of the CBI, urged British business to change the organisation of work to take account of what he called 'family-friendly' employment policies – ways of structuring work that allow employees to balance better their work and family commitments:[2]

> Business will not maximise its potential unless the skills and energies of all its people are given an opportunity to be developed and expressed. That means devising employment policies and working practices more compatible with family life.

How far can we go with flexibility?

Flexible working patterns may provide at least part of the answer to these dilemmas. The writer and commentator Michael Syrett[3] pointed out that flexibility and innovative working arrangements may often be the result of the needs of both employer and employee:

- the economic 'push' of organisations wishing to achieve competitive and cost-effective employment practices
- the social 'pull' of individuals who want greater control over their working hours and career development.

Some examples are given in Table 9.1.

An Institute of Management survey in 1994 predicted that the use of contracting out, work sharing and homeworking would increase by over 40 per cent. However, an even bigger increase was forecast in the use of older workers and flexible retirement (75 per cent), and of temporary workers (60 per cent).

Table 9.1   *Flexible work patterns*

Motivation	Appropriate work patterns
To cope with fluctuating levels of demand (economic)	Overtime, flexitime, temporary work, contract work (fixed term and fixed job), agency work
To reduce office overheads (economic)	Homeworking, agency and contract work
To make better use of capital equipment (economic)	Overtime, shiftworking, part-time work
To aid recruitment and retention (economic/social)	Career break schemes, job sharing, part-time, homeworking
To promote equal opportunities (social)	Career break schemes, job sharing, part-time, homeworking
To reward employees (social)	Sabbaticals
To enhance management development (economic/social)	Secondments, career break schemes

Source: Syrett 1989; reproduced by permission of Drake Beam Moric plc of Arlington Street, London SW1

A contribution from Europe.

The European Commission produced a paper in 1995 under the title of *Reconciliation of Professional and Family Life*. The paper derives from a number of related contexts. The first is equal opportunities. According to the Commission:

> ... there will be no substantial progress towards greater equality between men and women until a comprehensive reconciliation policy is put in place. It will be instrumental in relieving women in particular from unreasonable and conflicting demands in their working and family lives. It may also open up new employment opportunities for men and women.

The second context is:

> ... an integral part of the attempt to improve the functioning of European labour markets. Enabling workers to reconcile their family lives with their work obligations will allow more women to become economically active.

A third context is the family:

> The policy of reconciliation aims to uphold family relationships and responsibilities. The benefits for workers who can achieve greater harmony between their professional and family lives will be felt by their families too. As well as care of children, the question of care of the elderly and other family members with special needs also arises in this context. Men should be able to take a greater part in these caring arrangements.

Finally, training and education – the quality of Europe's human capital:

> In the face of ever-increasing levels of skill and expertise across the world, European workers need all possible support in upgrading their own skills.

Reconciliation could include training leave and sabbaticals.

The document concludes:

> It is submitted therefore that a policy rooted in equal opportunities has developed into one focused on quality. Quality of family life, quality of working life and quality of human resources.

Personnel – back to our roots?

The origins of personnel work stemmed from social needs. For the sake of the future of individual employees, the ultimate viability of their organisations and the health of society itself, it may be that the function needs in some way to return to these roots. Reading the future leads to the conclusion that designing ways to tackle the domestic challenges that confront us will be an important strategic task.

REGULATORY

Realism tells us that people – and organisations – are reluctant to change unless there are extremely good reasons to do so. In fact, one researcher is currently looking into the fact that they often do not change *even when they know it would be in their own interest to do so*. The European Commission probably believe that their initiative on reconciliation will only have a real impact if it is eventually enshrined in a Directive – and they may well be right.

Hence, grasping the importance of regulation and other similar pressures is integral to reading the future. According to the World Health Organisation, the UK is near the top of the world league table in terms of mortality due to heart disease. On the other hand, the United States is showing a substantial decline. Professor Cooper points out that this is not because US firms are becoming more altruistic and caring.[4] In fact, two trends are forcing American employers to take action. First, US industry is facing a vast bill for employee healthcare. Employers' healthcare insurance is now by far the largest element in employment costs apart from actual salary. Secondly, more and more employees in the US are litigating against their employers in respect of job-related stress. In California, there are now over 3000 cases each year of compensation claims for work-related psychiatric injury.

Regulating health and safety

In 1994, we saw the first cases in the UK of employees suing their employer for exposing them to stress, in breach of their statutory duty of care. In other words, the onus on employers to ensure that there are safe systems of work is now seen to encompass psychiatric risks as well as physical ones. This also affects the assessments of places of work and health and safety risks incumbent on employers under regulations introduced in January 1993.

The impact of Europe

These regulations did not result from a UK government initiative, but were implemented by a European Directive. Clearly, Europe represents a growing source of regulation and pressure in the social field. Any personnel manager who is serious about helping his or her employer to stay ahead of the game must have a really sound grasp of the European scene. It is not good enough to rely on the UK opt-out from the Social Chapter, for three reasons:

- The fact that the UK is technically outside the scope of a Directive is no guarantee that it will not impact UK employers. It is now clear for example that a great number of UK companies have little option but to establish European Works Councils.
- Employment related action on the part of the Commission will not necessarily be confined to steps under the Social Chapter. For instance, at the time of writing it seems unlikely that the UK government will win its appeal against the imposition of the Working Time Directive. If this is judged to be a legitimate health and safety measure, it will apply to this country as to the rest of the EU.
- Should there be a future Labour government, the UK will opt-in to the Social Chapter anyway.

The EU's social policy White Paper published in 1994 emphasised that its priorities had shifted to the adoption of minimum standards, and to ensuring that measures already on the statute book were implemented in practice by member states. Nevertheless, it envisages a substantial programme. One is tempted to say that if this is a minimalist programme, one dreads to think what a programme of fresh measures might have meant for employers – and for the workload of personnel practitioners.

In general terms, the main thrust focuses on unemployment and the social and economic integration of people currently excluded from the labour market. During the life of the new Commission, we can anticipate action in the following broad areas:

- *Employee information and consultation* Remember that this is against the background of the finding that the UK is in breach of statutory obligations by enabling employers to avoid consulting with employees where no trade union is recognised. We may be faced with a rethink of the whole basis of employee and union recognition and consultation.
- *Free movement* There are potential implications for the mobility of occupational pensions, and the availability of social security across national boundaries.

- *Education and training* We could see guarantees of education and training for young workers, and incentives or penalties to encourage the adoption of training standards.
- *Discrimination* The Commission wants a new legal basis in the EU treaties for legislation against discrimination on the grounds of race, religion, disability and age. A Charter of Social Rights for EU citizens may well be proposed.

UK pensions

The pensions field has long been a prime example of the impact of regulation, and is set fair to continue in that vein. It is a crucial issue for personnel in many ways. A sound approach to pensions is important in the ability to recruit and retain and pensions contributions represent a major element of cost in the employment package. Pensions administration is also heavy in cost. Yet too many personnel people have never come to grips with the subject. If we are to plan properly for the future, we need to understand both the current situation and the direction policy and regulation are likely to take in the future.

UK training

Training is another area where regulation of some kind could well be on the agenda. There has been general agreement that Britain has problems with the current skills level of its workforce, especially when compared with our rivals abroad. Regulation was first imposed in 1964 with the levy/grant system managed by Industrial Training Boards. In fact, the ITBs were only finally abolished in 1991.

Although it is generally recognised that progress has been made, particularly in the provision of further education, there is still unease as to whether the voluntary approach will deliver the goods. In 1994 the TUC published a consultative paper, *A New Partnership for Company Training*, and at the time of writing the IPD is reconsidering its position. Intervention in the training market is possible in a number of ways:

- *Economy-wide regulation*, as in health and safety training.
- *Industry specific regulations*, as laid down for example by the Building Societies Act.
- *The 'licence to practice'*. This is already well established for certain professions such as Chartered Surveyors and Accountants, and is

likely to be extended; continuing professional development schemes
are under way, not least of course for IPD members.

- *A training levy or tax rebate.* While there may not be widespread
  support for the old-style levy system, other approaches are available.
  The former IPM argued for a tax rebate, up to the level of 1 per cent
  of payroll, perhaps linked to employers' national insurance contributions.
- *The National Training Awards programme* is of course a form of
  intervention, albeit voluntary carrot rather than stick.
- Finally, some have argued that *the Investors in People standard* is a ready
  made vehicle for some form of quasi-regulatory intervention.

Corporate governance

With the establishment of the Cadbury Committee, the concept of
'corporate governance' became more than an arcane piece of jargon. The
purpose of the committee was to respond to concern that company
accounts often failed to present a picture of the company's finances that
shareholders could readily understand. Although its task was to study
the financial aspects of corporate governance, the committee's report
touched on other aspects of the way companies were governed, including
the role of non-executive directors and executive remuneration.

The report's recommendations were voluntary, but it was agreed that
a Cadbury Mark 2 would be set up in 1995 to examine compliance and
decide whether the existing measures do enough to improve standards of
corporate governance. What is at stake is the perception of business
among shareholders and the public at large. The aim is to achieve sufficiently high standards by voluntary regulation, with a view to avoiding
imposition by statute.

Some observers feel the recommendations do not go far enough. For
example, the National Association of Pension Funds would like to see the
maximum term of any director's contract shortened from three years to
one; it would also like shareholders to have better access to the full terms
of directors' contracts. The Association of British Insurers has requested
that the rationale for pay awards be fully disclosed.

The pay issue

In fact, the whole pay issue refuses to go away. A variety of cases
concerning top executive pay received publicity in early 1995, leading to

yet another committee. Author and company chairman Stanley Wright, dealing with the problems in *The Guardian*, wrote:[5]

> There is justifiable concern about high and rising levels of top executive pay which are often unrelated to achievement or performance. It is the most outrageous manifestation of inadequately accountable power, but also part of a wider problem of the accountability of managers.

Wright argued for a package of legal measures which went far beyond the Cadbury code.

Where does personnel come in?

Some readers may be feeling I am straying rather far from the brief about the role of personnel. Yet what could be more fundamental to human resource management than pay, training, contracts of employment and roles within organisations? It is a sad commentary on the function that in all the public furore about remuneration, the views of the professionals in the field were apparently totally disregarded.

Let's recap on two points:

- To win and retain strategic clout, personnel must be business oriented. This means, among other things, taking a close interest in, and understanding the impact of, all these crucial matters of regulation and governance.
- A fundamental part of being strategic is looking ahead, being ahead of the game, reading the future.

VISIONARY

We have looked at the future in terms of domestic and regulatory issues. What of our third category, the visionary? The personnel practitioner searching for clues about the future of business and his or her place in it, could do worse than look in the first instance to Professor Charles Handy:[6]

> Even those who lead lives far removed from the factories and shops of manufacturing and commerce need to have a view on business, who it is for and what it is for. Directly or indirectly, their economic well-being depends on it. A recession brings home to everyone the importance of a healthy trading sector in the economy. Does this mean however that business is purely a wealth-creating instrument, best left alone to do what

it has to do, or does it mean that, precisely because of its social impact, it has to recognise a wider accountability than making its owners seriously rich?

Handy poses two questions, 'what is business for?' and 'what is the nature of a company?' These questions are about the future because we are currently floundering between two concepts, as befits the approach of a millennium. The old concepts are past their sell-by dates, but hanging on – the new ones are hotly debated but not quite fully formed.

We need a new mental model of business activity

In these circumstances, it is not surprising that the personnel function is under pressure. It is faced with severe contradictions and is very much the meat in the proverbial sandwich. Look at two particular dilemmas:

- *Training* It is universally accepted that we must train or suffer the consequences – as a society, as a competitive economy and as separate businesses. Yet immediate pressures block us from doing a thoroughgoing job.
- *Motivation* Few would now argue with the proposition that people are crucial to successful enterprise. Yet they are still often treated in terms of the old-fashioned factors of production.

Personnel has to manage these and other related contradictions. This is not a comfortable place to be and it is perhaps not surprising if the function ends up with few friends. At the heart of these dilemmas lies the fact that past concepts of the purpose and organisation of business have broken down. Formerly, everyone knew and accepted that business was transacted on the basis of the stock company, owned and accountable to the shareholders, and directed by the board. Today, the legal framework no longer corresponds comfortably with reality. There is no longer an agreed 'mental model' as to how things should be done.

To press further the issue of motivation and commitment on the part of employees, those on whom business now depends. Is it really sensible to expect them to rally to the objective of making money for the shareholders? There is compelling evidence, let alone the evidence of common sense, that what means much more to people is the sense that they are producing a quality product or service that is valued by society and is worthwhile in its own right.

Yet management feels compelled to support the ritual declaration that 'we are in business to make money'. Anyone departing from this party line risks ridicule. Thorn EMI acquired the well-known bookshop chain, Dillon's. Chairman Sir Colin Southgate dared to refer to the cultural importance of bookselling and was immediately castigated by one financial journalist, who appeared to believe that Sir Colin's real cultural contribution would be his ability to cut distribution costs.

Handy recalled a dictum from the Watkinson Report 20 years ago on the responsibilities of the British public company: 'profits are the principal yardstick'. He goes on to comment:

> ... but a yardstick for what? And how can a yardstick be a purpose? It's like saying that you play cricket to get a good batting average. It's the wrong way round. You need a good average to keep on playing and to get into the first team. We need to clean up our logic.

Tomorrow's company

One initiative designed to look at the logic and point the way to the future is the RSA inquiry into *Tomorrow's Company: The Role of Business in a Changing World*. The objective was to develop a shared vision of tomorrow's company. In 1994 the inquiry produced its interim report. The report 'challenged business leaders to change their approach'. It set out its central concern as 'the achievement of sustainable business success in the face of continuing and substantial change in the nature and intensity of global competition'.

Among various considerations taken into account, two stand out:

- The nature of competition is changing as the interdependence increases between companies and the community. In order to be internationally competitive the company requires a supportive operating environment. The responsibility for maintaining this is shared between business, government and other partners who therefore need to develop a shared vision and a common agenda.
- The conventional wisdom in the UK is to define the purpose of business in terms that stress the importance of immediate financial performance and returns to shareholders, and treat other participants merely as means to this end. Of course, a board must continually attend to its company's financial performance and levels of shareholder return, but an *exclusive* concentration on any one stakeholder will not lead to sustainable competitive performance. It is therefore not necessarily in the best interests of shareholders to be singled out in this way.

The conclusion reached by the inquiry is that tomorrow's company must take an *inclusive* approach with customers, suppliers, employees, investors and the community. It elaborates:

> Under the inclusive approach, success is not defined in terms of a single bottom line, nor is purpose defined in terms of a single stakeholder. Tomorrow's company will understand and measure the value which it derives from all its key relationships. It will be well informed when it is confronted with the need to trade off the differing expectations of customers, suppliers, employees, investors and the communities in which it operates. This approach recognises the need for each company to choose its own model of critical business processes, and derive its own range of success measures.

The report sets out the main features of a company adopting the inclusive approach:

- It will be clear about its own distinctive purpose and values.
- It will give a lead in all its relationships by communicating its purpose and values in a consistent manner.
- It will recognise that all its relationships are reciprocal.
- It will see itself as part of a wider system.
- It will recognise the potential need to make trade-offs between stakeholders.
- It will recognise the need to measure and communicate its performance in all its relationships.

This interim report stimulated some debate; however the real test is yet to come as to whether the vision it sketches out has any hope of realisation. Nevertheless, it provides a powerful stimulus for the future thinking of personnel practitioners. For example:

- Professor Handy described the report as a 'shot in the arm', but felt it did not go far enough in tackling the big issue of key employees. Should not knowledge workers in the future company replace buildings and plant as its most important assets?
- One feature of the 'inclusive company' brought out by the inquiry was 'the need to learn fast and change fast'. This links with the idea of the learning organisation and innovation. In the 1993 Henley study of companies in the 'Golden Triangle' which focussed on growth and innovation, the creation of a learning organisation was seen as of relatively low importance; performance in that regard received an even lower rating. We have a long way to go!

- The interim report gave emphasis to measuring and communicating the company's performance with employees, as with other constituencies.

In the future, new ways of measuring?

As part of the process of the inquiry, the RSA created a network of interested people. One of these, consultant Alan Benjamin, tackled head on this issue of measuring and communicating, by producing an annual report for a hypothetical firm, Prototype plc.[7] The report includes measures of progress for all stakeholders, and one idea is that progress is assessed and reported on not only by management but by each stakeholder group itself. Among the key performance measures is 'value of knowledge bank', based on the proportion of employee costs, notably training and related activities, judged to generate future cash streams. An innovation ratio is shown, based on the relationship between expenditure on research, development, training and product branding and value added by employees.

A real life example is provided by the Social Audit produced annually by Traidcraft plc. Four pages of the 1993–4 audit are devoted to staff perspectives. Following the previous year's audit, the directors set targets against a number of ethical and social performance indicators. Performance in these areas was monitored and reported using the following sources:

- personnel department records
- reports by the staff association
- an external review of environmental issues at Traidcraft plc
- consultant's report *A Review of Corporate Spirituality*
- Tyneside TEC's *Investors in People* report.

These sources provided perspectives on matters including a fair wages policy, equality of opportunity, company culture, skills development, and health and safety.

This example may seem somewhat out of the main stream of business activity; in fact, it is an example of one organisation using a technique set out by Professor Robert Eccles in *Harvard Business Review*.[8] This employs what has become known as a scorecard of measures. The headings of such a scorecard might include the intellectual assets of the company (including brands, patents, and skill base), the customer, and the environment. Under each heading might be:

- intellectual assets – expenditure on asset enhancement, including R&D, training and recruitment of key skills.
- customer – quality, customer satisfaction, and customer retention rate.
- environment – investment in environmental improvement, community work, and relationship with relevant universities.

Potential impact of institutional shareholders

Another significant movement is so-called 'activism' by institutional shareholders. A leading example has been set by the California State Pension Fund, which has defined a range of performance criteria which it will use to determine those companies it will invest in – and these are not just financial criteria. There are signs that such an approach to investment may be developed among UK institutions. Given the enormous preponderance of pension funds and other institutions among UK shareholders, such a development would have huge implications. Suppose for example that the institutions accepted the findings of a Harvard study by Kotter and Heskett, which looked at connections between business success and culture. A clear conclusion was that:[9]

> ... firms whose cultures seem consistently to produce long-term economic success share one fundamental characteristic: their managers do not let the short-term interests of shareholders over-ride all else, but care equally about all of the company's stakeholders.

Suppose again that they accepted the conclusions of the study of corporate performance conducted by the University of Sheffield's Institute of Work Psychology[10]. The researchers examined innovation in various domains within participating firms, including new products, production technology, production process, work organisation and administrative practices. Initial findings suggest:

- Unionised companies are more innovative than non-unionised companies.
- Expenditure on training does not predict innovation, but having a training strategy and conducting training needs analyses do.
- Organisations rated highly by employees in relation to communication, vision, innovativeness, participation, skill development and inter-departmental relations have high levels of innovation.

The kind of visionary thinking about the future suggested in this section presents great opportunities for the personnel function – if we are prepared to take them.

Key questions

- What kind of changes do you foresee in your own reading of the future?
- What potential opportunities would arise from such changes?
- What do you need to do to ensure you will remain competent to operate in such a future?

Notes

1. Bridges, William *Jobshift*, see Bibliography.
2. *The Times* (1994) 'CBI wants work practices to be "family-friendly" ' 13 April p26.
3. Syrett, Michael (1989) *New Work Patterns: Matching Policy to Practice in the UK and other European Countries* Occasional Paper 90.2 Drake Beam Morin plc (DBM).
4. Cooper, Cary L (1993) *Managing Stress in the Workplace* Occasional Paper DBM.
5. Wright, Stanley (1994) 'How shareholders can put paid to inflated boardroom pay and egos' *The Guardian* 14 December.
6. Handy, Charles *The Empty Raincoat*, see Bibliography.
7. Benjamin, Alan (1994) *Prototype plc* Photogenesis Limited.
8. Eccles, Robert (1991) 'The performance measurement manifesto' *Harvard Business Review* Vol 69 No 1 January/February pp131–7.
9. Kotter, John and Heskett, James *Corporate Culture and Performance*, see Bibliography.
10. *Study of Corporate Performance in the UK Manufacturing Sector*, conducted by the Institute of Work Psychology of the University of Sheffield and the Institute of Economics and Statistics at the University of Oxford. Project Director, Professor Michael West – initial findings 1995.

Epilogue

"There is a tide in the affairs of men,
Which taken at the flood leads on to fortune;
Omitted, all the voyage of their life
Is bound in shallows and in miseries".
William Shakespeare

I have tried in this book to set out the opportunity and the challenge facing all of us in the personnel profession in the second half of the '90s – and beyond. As the writing has gone on, I have more and more concluded that moving down the strategic road means reinventing our function.

This means unlearning things, and letting go of our old power base. Of course there is risk in this, but if all we can do is to hold on to what we know we shall certainly end up in the shallows. At the very least we shall lose any real satisfaction – and miss out on a lot of fun!

Some concluding thoughts.

- It's no good waiting for the boss, or the company, to give a lead. There are things in this book that everyone can follow through at their own level. We know that if we don't act now, we shall be no further ahead in two years' time – and that means falling behind. This is the time to take responsibility for our own development. Above all, we must keep learning. Once we stop, it is time to move on.

- All personnel people must get a stint in line management, ideally early on in a career. If you are past that point, work out a strategy to enable you to spend some time out of the personnel role – heading up a task force or project team for example.

- Think big – the average spend on training of the Henley 'Golden

Triangle' companies was less than 2 per cent of revenue. This is a long way from world class. Hewlett-Packard was reported to spend more than three times as much.

- But move in small incremental steps. That's strategic!
- Above all, hang on to the abiding foundation that people do matter. Tom Peters wrote: 'relationships really are all there is'.

May I leave the final word to Charles Handy:[1]

> The world is up for reinvention in so many ways. Creativity is born in chaos. What we do, what we belong to, why we do it, when we do it, where we do it – these may all be different and they could be better. Change comes from small initiatives which work, initiatives which, imitated, become the fashion. We cannot wait for great visions from great people, for they are in short supply. It is up to us to light our own small fires in the darkness.

Notes

1.   Handy, Charles *The Empty Raincoat*, see Bibliography for Chapter 9.

Appendix

A strategic checklist for young managers

Here are six ways to develop your own strategic approach.

1. *Build personal effectiveness*
   — Learn the personal skills – consulting, negotiating, counselling, influencing, coaching, presentation and decision-making. Learn to monitor your own performance in your interactions with others.
   — Learn the business skills – especially understanding finance and accounts, and computer literacy.

2. *Learn about your business*
   — Opportunities to do this abound for personnel people, as you have every chance to move around all parts of the organisation. Be curious, ask questions about what's going on and why; showing a real interest always elicits a tremendous response. Also, follow press comment, read the Annual Report and other business reports that come your way: if you don't understand them, ask.

3. *Be strategic*
   — This means being proactive, building on your strengths, looking ahead, playing a role in professional circles, developing your network.

4. *Be flexible*
   — Don't hold on to old responsibilities, unlearn as the world changes; let go and hand over to the line where appropriate.

5. *Pay attention to internal public relations*
   — Make sure people know you are doing a good job.

6. *Have your own business plan*
    — Take responsibility for your own learning and development, be
      aware of the ways you add value to the business; make a note of
      your achievements, and take steps to quantify the value of work
      you do.

Bibliography

CHAPTER 1

Dixit, Avinash and Nalebuff, Barry (1991) *Thinking Strategically* W W Norton, London.

Kay, John (1993) *Foundations of Corporate Success* Oxford University Press, Oxford.

Kepner, Charles and Tregoe, Benjamin (1965) *The Rational Manager* McGraw-Hill, New York.

Mintzberg, Henry (1994) *The Rise and Fall of Strategic Planning* Prentice Hall, New Jersey.

Moore, J I (1993) *Writers on Strategy and Strategic Management: The Theory of Strategy and the Practice of Strategic Management at Enterprise, Corporate, Business and Functional Levels* Penguin Books, Harmondsworth.

Pascale, Richard (1991) *Managing on the Edge – how successful companies use conflict to stay ahead*, Penguin, Harmondsworth.

Quinn, James B and Mintzberg, Henry (1992) *The Strategy Process: Cases* Prentice Hall, New Jersey.

Rhodes, Jerry (1988) *The Colours of Your Mind* Collins.

Tregoe, B and Zimmerman, J (1980) *Top Management Strategy*, S&S Trade.

Welch, Barry (1992) *Managing to Make Organisations Work* Institute of Directors (IOD)

CHAPTER 2

Carlzon, Jan (1987) *Moments of Truth – New Strategies for To-day's Customer-Driven Economy* Ballinger Publishing.

Cartwright, Sue and Cooper, Cary (1992) *Mergers and Acquisitions: The Human Factors* Butterworth Heinemann, Oxford.

Drucker, Peter (1993) *Post-Capitalist Society* Butterworth Heinemann, Oxford.

Harvey, David (1994) 'Re-engineering: the Critical Success Factors' *Management Today* report.

Henley Management College/Price Waterhouse *The Golden Triangle Business Surveys* annual.

Naisbitt, John (1994) *Global Paradox: The Bigger the World Economy, the More Powerful its Smallest Players* Nicholas Brealey, London.

Rajan, Amin (1994) *Winning People* London Human Resource Group/CREATE.

CHAPTER 3

IBM/Towers Perrin (1992) *Priorities for Competitive Advantage – a 21st Century Vision* Towers Perrin.

Purcell, John and Ahlstrand, Bruce (1994) *Human Resource Management in the Multi-Divisional Company* Oxford University Press, Oxford.

CHAPTER 4

IMD (1992) *The Emerging Role of the HR Manager in Europe*, International Institute for Management Development (IMD) report prepared for the European Association for Personnel Management.

Schonberger, Richard (1990) *Building a Chain of Customers* Hutchinson, London.

Whiteley, Richard (1991) *The Customer Driven Company* Addison-Wesley, Wokingham.

CHAPTER 5

Armstrong, Michael (1995) *Handbook of Personnel Management Practice* Kogan Page, London.

Harvey-Jones, John (1992) *Trouble Shooter 2* BBC Books, London.

Simons, Robert (1994) *Levers of Control: How Managers Use Innovative Control Systems to Drive Strategic Renewal* Harvard Business School Press.

Starkey, Ken and McKinlay, Alan (1993) *Strategy and the Human Resource: Ford and the Search for Competitive Advantage* Blackwell, Oxford.

Tichy, Noel and Devanna, Mary Anne (1986) *The Transformational Leader* John Wiley, Chichester.

CHAPTER 6

Stewart, Rosemary (1982) *Choices for the Manager* McGraw-Hill, New York.

Tyson, Shaun and Fell, Alan (1986) *Evaluating the Personnel Function* Hutchinson, London.

CHAPTER 7

Barham, Kevin and Wills, Stefan (1992) *Management across Frontiers – identifying the competences of successful international managers*, Ashridge.

Hofstede, G (1984) *Culture's Consequences: international differences in work-related values* Sage, London.

Mayo, Andrew (1991) *Management Careers: Strategies for Organisations*, Institute of Personnel Management (IPM)

Millward, Neil, Stevens, Mark, Smart, David and Hawes, W R (1992) *Workplace Industrial Relations in Transition*, Dartmouth, Aldershot.

Thompson, Marc (1993) *Pay and Performance: the employees' experience* Institute of Manpower Studies.

Trompenaars, F (1993) *Riding the Waves of Culture* Nicholas Brealey, London.

CHAPTER 8

Hamel, G and Prahalad, C K (1994) *Competing for the Future* Harvard Business School Press.

CHAPTER 9

Bridges, William (1995) *Jobshift* Nicholas Brealey, London.

Cooper, Cary and Rachel (1988) *Living with Stress* Penguin, Harmondsworth.

Handy, Charles (1994) *The Empty Raincoat* Hutchinson, London.

Kotter, John and Heskett, James (1992) *Corporate Culture and Performance* The Free Press Macmillan Inc, New York.

RSA (The Royal Society for the encouragement of Arts, Manufactures & Commerce) (1994) *Tomorrow's Company: The Role of Business in a Changing World RSA inquiry, interim report.*

Index